Margaret Laurence and Her Works

Margaret Laurence (1926–87)

J. M. KERTZER

Biography

> A novel based on a writer's experience is no less a work of true fiction than a novel which has nothing to do with the writer's own life. The art of fiction lies in the ability to bring to life on the printed page a whole range of characters and events, and to explore meaningful and universal themes. In this sense it has nothing to do with simply recording the events of anyone's life.[1]

MARGARET LAURENCE'S fiction is neither autobiographical nor confessional, though it does incorporate many features from her own life: her youth, family heritage, and upbringing in Manitoba; her travels through Canada, Europe, and Africa; her struggles as a Canadian, woman writer. But as her comment shows, she regarded a novel, not as a disguised recording of its author's experience, but as a separate creation with a life of its own. It is a "work of true fiction," a well-crafted story whose truth is in its telling and in the vitality of its characters, not in its correspondence to fact. She warns us, therefore, about interpreting novels biographically by seeking conformity between an author and her work. Nevertheless, we are justified in considering Laurence's life for its own interest — it was eventful and even adventurous — and for the light it casts on her aims, convictions, interests, and habits as a novelist. It helps us understand the temperament of a temperamental writer, that is, of a writer whose main interest lay in the complexities and nuances of human character.

Jean Margaret Wemyss was born on 18 July 1926 in Neepawa, Manitoba, the daughter of Robert and Verna Simpson Wemyss. She came from a family of respectable lawyers, craftsmen, and merchants who were of Scottish and Irish stock. Of her Celtic heritage she has written both affectionately and critically, finding it colourful, proud, clannish, snobbish, and Presbyterian. She notes its obsession with hard work, discipline, guilt, and with the "Black Celt" feeling "that things could hardly be worse in the world, and that we are on the brink of a precipice."[2] She has also written of Neepawa, which became her fictional Manawaka, as a town at once protective, splendid, and stultifying. It first directed her vision of the world and therefore "would form the mainspring and source of the writing [she] was to do, wherever and however far away [she] might live."[3] After her mother died in 1930, and her father in 1935, she was raised by her maternal grandfather, John Simpson, and by her aunt, Margaret Simpson Wemyss, who had married her widowed father. Both were strong influences on the young girl. The spirit of John Simpson, a repressive, authoritarian figure who was a cabinet-maker and undertaker, haunts many of Laurence's novels. He appears as Timothy Connor in *A Bird in the House*. The fictional Vanessa says of him, as did Laurence of her grandfather: "I had feared and fought the old man, yet he proclaimed himself in my veins."[4] Her aunt and stepmother was an intelligent woman, a teacher, and founder of the Neepawa Public Library. She encouraged Laurence to read, and the girl started writing by the age of six or seven, though it was not until she was about twenty-three that she took herself seriously as a writer.

She lived in Neepawa through the depression and World War II until 1944, when she attended United College in Winnipeg. There she studied English, published her first poems and stories in the college journal, *Vox*, and later worked as a reporter for *The Winnipeg Citizen*. In these formative years, according to Clara Thomas, she responded to the "powerfully positive, liberal idealism" of the college, and to the optimism of the "Winnipeg Old Left," with its confidence in reform, brotherhood, and social justice.[5] Laurence later questioned her easy liberal attitudes, which were sorely tried in Africa, but she retained her indignation with forms of injustice, exploitation, and dispossession, though she grew sceptical of social solutions. She retained the compassionate, moral outlook that pervades her novels.

In Winnipeg she also met her husband, Jack Laurence, a civil engineer. They married in 1948 and proceeded first to England and then in 1950 to the British Protectorate of Somaliland in East Africa. In primitive and often dangerous conditions, he supervised the construction of a series of reservoirs in the desert. Meanwhile she immersed herself in Somali culture, as far as was permissable for a foreign woman; she later recorded and interpreted her experiences in

The Prophet's Camel Bell (1963). At the time, her main project was to study the oral tradition of Somali literature and to prepare a book of translations, *A Tree for Poverty* (1954). This was her first published volume, and it is hard to imagine anything further from Neepawa in place and spirit than the *belwo* and *gabei*, the lyrical and narrative poems in this book. Between 1952 and 1957, the Laurences lived in the Gold Coast, later Ghana, where they had two children, Jocelyn (born 1952) and David (born 1955). Her career as a writer of fiction began at this time as she wrote stories about the life that she observed around her. She published her first African story, "The Drummer of All the World," in *Queen's Quarterly* in 1956 and wrote several others later included in *The Tomorrow-Tamer* (1963). She also began her first and only African novel, *This Side Jordan* (1960). These years in Africa were of enormous importance to her development as a writer, and therefore I will consider their influence at length in the next section. At this point it is sufficient to note that they affected her long after she left Africa because she continued to read and learn from the work of talented Nigerian novelists and dramatists. Her critical study of them, *Long Drums and Cannons: Nigerian Dramatists and Novelists 1952–1966* (1968), while valuable in itself, is also interesting because it offers insight into her own books and displays her views of the art of fiction.

In 1957 the Laurences moved to Vancouver, where Margaret completed *This Side Jordan*, which won the Beta Sigma Phi Award for the best first novel by a Canadian, and began *The Stone Angel*. In her second novel, she returned to her native ground and took the most important step in her career:

> When I stopped writing about Africa and turned to the area of writing where I most wanted to be, my own people and background, I felt very hesitant. The character of Hagar had been in mind for quite a while before I summoned enough nerve to begin the novel. Strangely enough, however, once I began *The Stone Angel*, it wrote itself more easily than anything I have ever done. I experienced the enormous pleasure of coming home in terms of idiom.[6]

In her own life, however, she had not yet come home. She seems to have needed a more distant view of herself, her country, and her art, and so in 1962, after separating from her husband, she took her manuscript and her children to England. She lived at Elm Cottage in Buckinghamshire. Here she created the world of Manawaka, completing *The Stone Angel* (1964) and writing *A Jest of God* (1966), which won the Governor General's Award, *The Fire-Dwellers* (1969), and *A Bird in the House* (1970). She also wrote her first children's book, *Jason's Quest* (1970). It was in England that she established herself as a major Canadian novelist and as a woman of letters, reading widely in Canadian literature, writing reviews, essays, and articles, and meeting other Canadian writers who visited her at Elm Cottage. "Her house," recalls Margaret Atwood, "was a rambling country-village cottage outside London whose chief characteristics were its multitude of books and its resemblance to Canada House at the height of the tourist season."[7]

Gradually Laurence was lured back to Canada. Through the 1970s, she was awarded honorary degrees from eleven Canadian universities; in 1971 she became a Companion of the Order of Canada; she served as writer-in-residence at Trent University and at the universities of Toronto and Western Ontario. She returned, first in summers to a cottage on the Otonobee River in Ontario, where she wrote much of *The Diviners* (1974), which won the Governor General's Award, and then permanently to the nearby town of Lakefield. She wrote three more children's books: *The Olden Days Coat* (1979), *Six Darn Cows* (1979), and *The Christmas Birthday Story* (1980). She spoke publicly on social issues, especially nuclear disarmament, proclaiming herself "a Christian, a woman, a writer, a parent, a member of humanity and a sharer in life itself, a life I believe to be informed and infused with the holy spirit."[8] In 1981 she was appointed Chancellor of Trent University, which is located in the very city, Peterborough, where a few upright citizens declared *The Diviners* to be an immoral book that should be removed from the high-school curriculum. Laurence died on 5 January 1987.

Tradition and Milieu

Despite her travels and devotion to foreign literature, Margaret Laurence has become, through her own efforts and the commentary of critics, one of the most important and most Canadian of novelists. Yet she admits that there "is certainly no sense of nationalism in a political sense in my work,"[9] and she excludes propaganda and didactic motives from a work of art.[10] Instead, she argues, writers are native to a specific place because they root themselves in its soil. They must deal, not with political or social abstractions, but with local, sensuous particulars: the "feel of place, the tone of speech, how people say things, the concepts you grow up with."[11] All larger themes will grow from this soil. For this reason she considers herself, not just a Canadian novelist, but a Prairie novelist. Neepawa remains the mainspring and source of her writing, and she counts as important early influences authors like Sinclair Ross and W. O. Mitchell, who excel in conveying the earthy feel of Prairie life. She experienced a "thrill of recognition" when she first read *Jake and the Kid* because ". . . these stories were among the first that many of us who lived on the prairies had ever read concerning our own people, our own place and our own time."[12]

It was a circuitous path, however, that took her from the real Neepawa to the literary Manawaka, the town which appears in her novels, and which she has built into an elaborate imaginative world. She had to be shocked and stimulated by the very different worlds of Somaliland, Ghana, and England before she could write about her home. Yet even this path, she told Robert Kroetsch, this "split desire to go or to stay . . . is a very western thing"; ". . . people have to go away and go through the process of learning about the rest of the world, and then they have to return"; only then can they come to terms with their "roots," their "ancestors," and their "gods."[13] In *The Diviners*, Morag makes the same discovery when she goes on a pilgrimage to what she assumes is her native Scotland, only to realize that her true home is in Manawaka. Laurence herself enjoyed a "seven years' love affair" with Africa ("Ten Years' Sentences," p. 18).

She found Africa totally alien and strangely familiar. Paradoxically, this exotic milieu allowed her to take a leading place within a Canadian literary tradition. Africa inspired her to write, first of all, by providing her with the rich and even fierce details that are the first element of fiction. As she describes it, Africa is a land of brilliant primary colours:

> At mid-morning the chop-bar was almost deserted. The proprietor, bulging with beery flesh under his dirty white trousers and green striped pyjama top, was washing glasses in a tin basin enamelled with overblown carnations. Above the bottles of Blood Wine, Iron Wine, orange squash, grenadine and gin

> on the shelves, corpulent blue flies buzzed lazy and slow, like old drunks without the price of solace.[14]

Such observations convey the "feel of place": they create and animate a fictional world. Laurence's Ghanaian stories are vibrant with the passion and confusion of the years preceding political independence. Although she later depicted the more muted shades of Western Canada, she remained committed to precise perception, vividly recorded. Perhaps she was first stimulated by the power of sensuous literary detail in Africa, where the senses are overwhelmed.

Africa also posed in particularly acute form the dilemma of understanding and portraying character. This was to become the goal of her novels. For Laurence, novelists require, first, a good eye, but second, an imaginative sympathy allowing them to enter into the personalities of their characters. As she describes her technique: "I take on, for the time I'm writing, the *persona* of the character, and I am trying to make a kind of direct connection with this person, not to manipulate them, but to listen to them, and to try and feel my way into their skull" (Cameron, pp. 102–03). But in Africa, the gap between cultures was so wide that she could hardly listen to people — though she did study their language — let alone make a direct connection. Therefore her chief literary ambition was both provoked and challenged by Africa. We see her confronting the dilemma in *The Prophet's Camel Bell*; the account of her sojourn in Somaliland is really about her continually frustrated efforts to make contact with the Somalis. To this end, she parades her liberal attitudes, befriends and teaches them, and studies their culture, history, and literature. She probes incidents for clues to the Somali state of mind. "My difficulty," she admits, "was in discovering how the tribesmen actually looked at things, for without a knowledge of basic concepts, communication is impossibly confused."[15] The book culminates in a series of character sketches, which study the personalities of the Africans she knew best. The sketches rely on interpretation and analysis, but also on description, dialogue, and the detailed recounting of scenes. They dramatize the elusive personalities in question by resorting to literary means. In short, they are sketches for a novel.

Finally, Africa offered Laurence her major themes. Her African stories, essays, and articles explore the issues of tribalism, colonialism, racial intolerance, betrayal, independence, the clash of generations, self-sacrifice, and survival in a harsh land — all subjects which recur, appropriately modified, in her Canadian novels. In the vibrant atmosphere of Africa, these problems appear particularly dramatic. What she later treated figuratively was literally true in Africa. For example, she frequently refers to a person's need to make peace with his or her past, ancestors, and gods; all her characters face this dilemma. In *The Diviners*, Morag finally does so emotionally and psychologically, but in Africa the gods are real, and the ancestors are actually present in the voice of the drums. We find a man like Moki, a minor character in "A Gourdful of Glory": "No one knew where Moki came from. He didn't know himself. He knew the name of his village, but not the country where it was, and he knew the names of his people's gods" (*TT*, pp. 228). Morag knows her town to be Manawaka, but she has to discover that her own country is Canada rather than Scotland, and that she owes allegiance to both Canadian and Scottish family gods. She accomplishes only figuratively what Moki must do literally. Thus Africa externalized in its vivid details and personalities what would later be the inward dilemmas of Laurence's heroines. It made visible for her "the dark continent of the mind, where the archetypal struggles take place between fathers and sons, matriarchs and their children, the living and the dead but ever-present ancestors, man and his gods, that area of the mind in which we are all forever seeking to re-film in fantasy our own pasts."[16]

When Laurence returned to Canada in 1957, still engaged in writing *This Side Jordan*, she saw her own country in the light of her years spent abroad. In particular, she observed three dilemmas that now fell into alignment. The first, prompted by seeing Africans face an abrupt and bewildering transition from traditional to modern eras, was the twin problem of freedom and survival, of gaining and maintaining "an independence which was both political and inner."[17] How can individuals live freely, at ease with themselves, their past, and the lives of others? This question immediately raised a second, for the private life responds to a thousand social pressures, some obvious, some insidious. How can individuals even assess their lives fairly when standards of judgement are imposed on them? Canada, like Africa, was "a land that had been a colony, a land which in some ways was still colonial. My people's standards of correctness and validity and excellence were still at that time largely derived from external and imposed values; our view of ourselves was still struggling against two other cultures' definitions of us" ("Ivory Tower or Grassroots?" pp. 22–23). The problem of colonialism seldom appears openly or politically in Laurence's Canadian fiction. Instead, it is implied in the habits, instincts, even turns of speech of her characters, in their numbing sense that their lives are not their own, and in their recurring need to escape from "correctness," often by retreating into the Canadian wilderness, far from social pressures and prejudices. The colonial mentality corresponded to a third problem that became apparent when Laurence began writing *The Stone Angel*. This was her "growing awareness of the dilemma and powerlessness of women, the tendency of women to accept male definitions of [themselves], to be self-deprecating and uncertain, and to rage inwardly" ("Ivory Tower or Grassroots?" p. 24). This is a different kind of colonialism that makes the issues of freedom and survival particularly acute for women. Laurence observed this condition in its starkest form in Somaliland, where women's lives are strictly scrutinized and directed by men, yet are romanticized elaborately in literature. She continued her observations in Canada, and while she has declared that she is "90% in agreement with Women's Lib,"[18] she is a thoroughly feminist writer in the sense that she explores sympathetically and critically the plight of women in twentieth-century Canada. She has written a history of this condition through four generations, from Hagar to Morag's daughter, Pique.

Freedom, survival, colonialism (or forms of coercion), and the plight of women were subjects for which Laurence had to find an appropriate literary form. The narrative strategy that she adopted and has continued to refine was indicated first in her African story "The Rain Child."[19] Its two main figures are women — whereas most of the early stories deal with men — who are culturally displaced and confounded by conflicting standards of female behaviour. The African girl raised in England feels herself a foreigner in her native land; the English woman in Ghana feels herself a stranger teaching an alien language to Africans. More important, for the first time Laurence uses a first-person, female narrator. Ironically self-critical, Violet Nedden talks about her unfortunate pupil, but in the process displays her own character and disillusionment. She looks forward to Laurence's Canadian women, who also speak in distinctive voices, thereby revealing more about themselves than they recognize.

With this story and this narrator, Laurence turned to the tradition of the modern psychological novel. She has shown little interest in the more radical, disruptive experiments of modern fiction. More conservatively, she has adopted, polished, and made her own, conventions established by early modern novelists like Henry James. His novels portray the "quality of inward life" of characters by dramatizing the operation of their minds. The hero is a "vessel of sensibility"; the novel charts his or her emotional and intellectual ordeal. Incident, dialogue, setting — all the outward or objective interests of the novel — become secondary to its subjective intent.[20] Laurence calls this form the "Method novel" (Cameron, p. 102), after the example of method acting: the author inhabits his or her characters and takes on their personalities. She contrasts her method with the broader social realism of Hugh MacLennan, Morley Callaghan, Ernest Buckler, and Sinclair Ross, an earlier generation of novelists who analyzed "the whole social pattern" (Cameron, p. 103). She aims instead at "the whole exploration of personality" (Cameron, p. 104), and social concerns, while never absent from her novels, appear only as they impinge on individual lives.

To the cosmopolitan example of James, Laurence added a good measure of Prairie realism. This is one of the main currents of Canadian fiction, stretching back to the works of Robert J. C. Stead and Frederick Philip Grove. Prairie novels often present realistic, detailed accounts of everyday life, tracing the settlement of the West from pioneering to farming to small-town life. Often they do so in a "chronicle" that follows the fortunes of a family. These are rural novels, set far from urban centres, to which they look with both distrust and longing. They retain, even in recent works, a strong sense of the frontier. Unlike the sophisticated Jamesian novel, they study the primitive encounter between man and nature: their characters respond to a vast, fertile, but often alien and oppressive landscape. The least common denominators of nature, the skeletal requirements of land and sky, as W. O. Mitchell calls them, dominate these novels. Therefore they often present, according to Dick Harrison, "a darker view of prairie experience" than earlier, sentimental fiction, even a tragic view that "conveys a painful sense of the human failure and waste, weakness and suffering." Alienation from the land and the failure of imagination are common themes, as man is undone by the very powers of body and mind through which he seeks to dominate his environment.[21] These conditions and themes appear in

Laurence's work as well. Clearly she owes much to this tradition in her depiction of Manawaka, its history, its proud families, and its assertive individuals. Yet Prairie clannishness corresponds to African tribalism, and even when depicting her native milieu in accordance with Canadian traditions, Laurence exhibits the influence of Africa.

Critical Overview and Context

Margaret Laurence's novels are intricate yet economical. Imagery, allusion, dialogue, and description all fall into a clear design. Nothing is extraneous. Each book is a self-sufficient whole that also participates in one of the two larger groupings — the African stories and the Manawaka cycle. In short, she is the kind of novelist that critics love. She invites the patient analysis of all she has so patiently constructed. Her novels yield separately to the subtle dissection of theme and technique, while her work as a whole provides a consistent vision for critics to elaborate. Consequently, there is a large, ever-growing body of criticism. Any serious student should consult first *The Annotated Bibliography of Canada's Major Authors*, in which Susan J. Warwick lists and describes 149 books, articles, interviews, and dissertations, as well as 86 selected reviews. I have listed a few more recent articles in the bibliography to this essay.

Because there is so much criticism, in the following pages I have reduced it to three major categories: studies of background, of character, and of narrative technique. These three necessarily overlap and fail to do justice to the variety of critical styles and approaches, but they do indicate the general shape of Laurence criticism. Before proceeding, however, I must draw attention to Clara Thomas, who has been Laurence's most prolific, sympathetic, and enthusiastic commentator. She has written two books as well as numerous essays, introductions, and lectures, which fall in and across all three critical categories. Her name will recur in the discussion that follows. Most extensive is *The Manawaka World of Margaret Laurence*, which is valuable for its biographical information and its close analysis of theme, character, and style. Another book-length study is Patricia Morley's *Margaret Laurence*, which follows the Twayne's World Authors format of biography, background, and exposition. Morley compares and integrates the two cycles (African and Canadian) of Laurence's work by distinguishing a controlling quest structure — a "psychic journey towards inner freedom and spiritual maturity."[22] Through this motif, all of Laurence's writing contributes to an epic vision that pairs tradition and development, native and foreign, family and stranger. I will consider this thematic pattern in a moment. A third book has recently been published by the University of Victoria Press, *Mother and Daughter Relationships in the Manawaka Novels of Margaret Laurence* (1985), by Helen M. Buss. The publisher describes it as a "Jungian archetypal approach to explore the development of Margaret Laurence's mother-daughter relationships."

Early reviews and articles on Laurence were often biographical, as they sought to introduce a new Canadian author and to discover how her character and background were reflected in her work. Joan Hind-Smith's *Three Voices* is an example of this approach.[23] Criticism dealing with background quickly moved in several divergent directions. Interest in Laurence the person, writer, or Canadian led to a series of interviews in which she talked freely about herself and her life. In the best of these, recorded by Clara Thomas, Donald Cameron, Graeme Gibson, Bernice Lever, Alan Twigg, Rosemary Sullivan, and Michel Fabre, she speaks about fiction in general and its power to depict character, and about her abiding interest in Canadian literature and its ability to shape our perception of the land and of ourselves. She tells about growing up in Neepawa, and how town and prairie worked themselves into her instincts and outlook. And she tells about the composition, aims, and sources of her novels.

Interest in Laurence's African background has prompted analysis of her early stories, of the continuity between them and her Canadian works, and of the ways that Africa inspired and directed her imagination. Critics such as S. E. Read, Henry Kreisel (both in *ML*), G. D. Killam, Clara Thomas, and Patricia Morley study themes of colonialism, freedom, ancestry, tribalism, betrayal, and lost innocence. Killam and Thomas judge Laurence's first efforts to express these subjects through credible characters living in and reacting to a colourful setting, and to establish a narrative stance permitting both intimacy and ironic detachment. Others consider Africa itself as subject or symbol. George Woodcock (*JCS*) and again Patricia Morley discuss her nonfiction, how she presents herself confronting Africa and its people, and how her experience as a foreigner influenced her novels set in her native land. Jane Leney (*JCF*) studies pastoralism as an aspect of colonialism, its psychology and literary depiction.

Patricia Monk argues that Canadian writers, including Laurence, treat Africa like a Jungian archetype, so that Africa serves as the "Shadow" of Canada.

Interest in Laurence's Prairie background has encouraged a major field of criticism examining the many ways in which the landscape and history of the Canadian West participate in her novels. The terms *setting* and *background*, suggesting something of secondary importance, give a mistaken impression of their full significance. The town of Manawaka, for example, is of primary interest to many critics who examine its historical, social, and symbolic functions. Thomas entitles one chapter of *The Manawaka World of Margaret Laurence* "The Town — Our Tribe" and gives the most complete tour and history of the town; she also relates it to pioneer experience and the settling of the West. Allan Bevan (*ML*), David Blewett, and John Lennox (both in *JCS*) consider the tight social order which both traps and sustains Laurence's heroines, while Kenneth Hughes (*JCS*) gives a political reading of *A Jest of God*, showing that Rachel, like Manawaka, displays the conditions of Canada in a post-colonial period. Moving outside the town into the countryside, critics such as Cathy N. Davidson, Leona Gom, Bernice Lever, Anne Thompson, and again Clara Thomas study the treatment of nature and natural imagery. They discuss the sense of place that pervades the novels, where the prairie, depicted as either wilderness or garden, provides a focus for opposing values. The landscape, by its very nature, suggests a moral or psychological drama in which characters and the town itself engage. Similarly, D. G. Jones, Margaret Atwood, and Dennis Cooley contrast the fierce vitality of the wilderness with the stultifying garrison culture of the town. This line of criticism owes a debt to Northrop Frye's famous essay in the second edition of the *Literary History of Canada*, as do the studies of Western Puritanism by William H. New, Dick Harrison, Laurence Ricou, and Sandra Djwa (*ML*), and by Leslie Monkman, Linda Hutcheon, and André Dommergues (all in *EC*). These consider the repressed states of mind encouraged by a small, isolated, fundamentalist society engulfed by a hostile environment. Djwa shows how the prairie resembles an Old Testament landscape, which punishes the tribal, patriarchal society that dares to inhabit it. Laurence has acknowledged the influence of this tradition of grim Prairie realism, praising Sinclair Ross in particular. But she has also commended W. O. Mitchell and the complementary tradition of Prairie romanticism, which stresses the garden rather than the wilderness. Edward McCourt, Dick Harrison, and Laurence Ricou, who set Laurence within the larger history of Prairie fiction, discuss both sides of the issue. Woodcock and Thomas claim that Laurence advances beyond realism to create myths of the West.

Laurence has declared frequently that her main purpose is the portrayal of human character: she dramatizes the temperament, voice, and evolving consciousness of a series of striking individuals. Consequently, critical attention often focuses on her treatment of character. These studies are the most common of all, and they are usually thematic and psychological in emphasis. Different commentators treat the recurring psychological patterns of the novels in different terms, but all agree that charting the characters' development and explaining the literary means used to express their progress are the main critical tasks. Laurence's protagonists review their lives in order to advance from ignorance, diffidence, and denial to knowledge, confidence, and affirmation. For S. E. Read (*ML*), this is the maze of life; for Walter Swayze, an odyssey; for Eleanor Johnston, a quest; for Patricia Morley, a journey of self-discovery; for C. M. McLay, an exploration of isolation and the attempt to overcome it; for Theo Q. Dombrowski, a search for identity and the forces that both define and obscure the self; for Clara Thomas, it is variously a double journey, a conversion fable, and a spiritual quest. These metaphors, all suggested by Laurence herself, indicate the form and the meaning of her novels. Other critics turn to Carl Jung for their vocabulary: Nancy Bailey, Angelika Maeser (*JCF*), Helen M. Buss, and Dennis Cooley analyze personality with the aid of Jungian psychology and examine the characters' development as a process of "individuation." The analysis of mythological and biblical allusions is another means of studying character and relating it to literary technique. Laurence is fond of legendary and biblical names, echoes, images, and quotations, all of which she uses to provide a psychological and dramatic commentary on her stories. With their aid, the novels trace a kind of pilgrim's progress from a state of desolate exile towards regeneration and revelation, from banishment in the wilderness towards the glory of Jerusalem. Djwa (*ML*), Thomas, New, and Claudette Pollack explicate the biblical names, archetypal associations, and literary references through which Laurence portrays the moral and emotional dilemmas of her protagonists. They prove that, far from making the occasional allusion, she weaves them intricately into the form, theme, and texture of her novels. Following a similar approach, Blewett (*JCS*) discusses "waste-land" images drawn from T. S. Eliot. Frank Pesando explains the balanced references to Genesis and Revelation, which provide a mythological framework of birth and death. Kenneth C. Russell discloses a providential pattern and gives the most strongly religious reading of the novels. David L. Jeffrey, most elaborately, examines how Laurence incorporated biblical hermeneutical models into the narrative and rhetorical structure of *The Stone Angel*.

Another group of critics studies Laurence's portrayal of women. While the African stories usually present men in the central roles, all the Canadian novels have heroines whose problems arise from being Western Canadian women. All three terms have received attention. Thomas examines the portrayal of pioneer women, and compares them to similar figures in Willa Cather, Nellie McClung, and Laura Salverson. John Moss, Lydia Burton, and David Morley consider the relation between the sexes; while Lois Gottlieb and Wendy Keitner, Denyse Forman and Uma Parameswaren (*ML*), and Helen M. Buss stress the relation between mothers and daughters and examine the treatment of motherhood. Judy Kearns (*JCF*), Margaret Atwood, and Isabel McKenna are interested in various literary and social female types, which reflect the ways men regard women and women regard themselves. Given the power and intricacy of Laurence's heroines, one would expect more criticism from a feminist point of view. In two such studies, Constance Rooke examines *The Stone Angel* as a battle with a patriarchal society and with the Victorian "angel in the house" image associated with women; and Stephanie A. Demetrakopoulos shows how Laurence treats the feminine as the "ground of being,"[24] by deftly reversing the female archetypes of Aphrodite, Artemis, Medusa, and Arachne.

Psychological analysis tends to be thematic, but it necessarily recognizes technique when considering how character development is registered in patterns of symbols, images, myths, or motifs. Several critics already noted, such as Jeffrey, Djwa, Dombrowski (and Linda Hutcheon, who studies Laurence's use of imagery), give close attention to technique. Nevertheless, I propose a third category, criticism of narrative technique, in order to distinguish those commentators who concentrate less on character than on style. They examine how a story is told, rather than whom the story describes.

My own discussion in the next section will also be of this kind, and will build on the work noted here.

Because Laurence's novels are all narrated either by their protagonists or in a manner that adopts their perspective and tone, the narrative voice is essential to the style and form of their stories. George Bowering (*ML*) and John Lennox (*JCS*) discuss this "vocal style," while Thomas, New, and Simone Vauthier (*EC*) are especially good at analyzing selected passages to show how patterns of speech direct the reader's attention, structure the novels, and offer insight into personality and into the whole world of Manawaka. Because the novels are essentially monologues, the speaking or meditating voice provides us with a distinctive perception of reality (Killam) that depends on the sensibility and reliability of the first-person narrator (Gom), who reviews and reassesses the past. The past is a lingering presence in the narrator's mind. He or she must disentangle a network of temporal pressures from personal and ancestral pasts, from family inheritance, from historical and legendary traditions (Melanie Mortlock [*JCF*], New, Gom, Sherrill Grace). Time itself becomes integral to Laurence's themes and techniques. Because the stories are told in retrospect, the very act of recalling enters into the drama, making memory an important structural principle (Davidson, Barbara Hehner, Reingard Nischik [*EC*]), a means of both recognition and deception (Dombrowski, Gom), and a power for integrating past and present in a meaningful whole (Grace, Pierre Spriet [*EC*]). Memory becomes a creative power that artfully surveys the past. *The Diviners* especially, whose narrator is also a writer, becomes a novel about fiction and the creative process (Ildikó de Papp Carrington, Cheryl Cooper). It displays the ambiguous interdependence of word, fiction, fact, truth, and conviction — all providing the shifting ground on which the novelist builds her "book of life" (Fabre).

Laurence's Works

> . . . my work resides in my fiction, which must always feel easy with paradox and accommodate contradictions, and which must, if anything, proclaim the human individual, unique and irreplaceable, and the human spirit, amazingly strong and yet in need of strength and grace. ("Ivory Tower or Grassroots?" p. 23)

There is great consistency in Margaret Laurence's reviews and articles on the nature of fiction and on her own work in particular. Although she displayed a certain reserve, especially in interviews, her comments show that she thought carefully about literature, that her judgement and tastes were formed, and that she had strong convictions about her duties, powers, and weaknesses as a writer. The above quotation is characteristic of her more formal pronouncements and offers a convenient avenue into her art. First, her work resides in fiction, that is, in the craft of storytelling. She delighted in the well-made novel – another legacy of Henry James – and, as Clara Thomas notes, from her earliest days, Laurence was a self-conscious, painstaking artist: "She has always been a 'literary' writer in the pattern of her works and allusions, in her experiments with form and voice, and supremely so in her ability to stand back, to look at her writing, and to describe the processes of its creation with both analytic precision and critical perception."[25] This analytic power is apparent in her criticism of Jack Ludwig for defying his own technique in *Above Ground* by allowing his first-person narrator to report the thoughts of another character; this lapse threatens "both the narrative flow and the authenticity of the single voice."[26] And it is apparent in her criticism of Chinua Achebe's *A Man of the People*; despite the book's accuracy in foreseeing the *coup d'état* in Nigeria, Laurence remained critical: "The fact that it actually happened this way in real life does not alter the impression that the novel ends rather too conveniently."[27] In both cases, her objection is on the grounds of literary craft. The novels are imperfectly made, inconsistent, or unconvincing. Flaws that to the less demanding reader might seem unimportant were seen by Laurence as serious faults because they undermine the authority of the whole artifice that rests on them.

That artifice must easily and eloquently "accommodate contradictions." Laurence regarded the novel as an artefact that holds, balances, and resolves opposing impulses. More simply, the novel is dramatic. It is a "vessel," not only in the sense that it is a containing form, but also in that it is a vehicle, a "vessel capable of risking that peculiar voyage of exploration which constitutes a novel."[28] Development through conflict is essential to it because it portrays the "human individual" who is inherently paradoxical, amazingly strong yet often weak, the source of both wonder and pity. It celebrates his or her uniqueness by exploring his or her innermost being. All Laurence's work proclaims "that there is a core, not just a surface" to life,[29] and that core is lodged in the "human spirit." She would have agreed with Virginia Woolf's famous assertion that the novel exists above all to express character because only there can the drama of life, and reality itself, be seized. For Laurence too, the novel strives "to catch vast and elusive life,"[30] "to put down life or one's consciousness or a character's consciousness" of it.[31] Because life *is* consciousness, fiction must dramatize the intimate, vital, contradictory workings of the human mind.

Given these premises, we can understand why Laurence admired novels whose characters are vivacious. Her highest praise was to say that a person "is a genuine fictional creation, someone who leaves the printed page and lives on in the mind."[32] Note the paradox here: characters leave the page not because they are real but because they are genuine fictions, because their creator has the literary skill to give a perfect illusion of life. The strength of the illusion convinces us that we actually know an imaginary person, and Laurence's greatest talent was to animate her work with such compelling fictions — her characters. In a revealing description of Jagua, heroine of a novel by Cyprian Ekwensi, we see the power and vitality that Laurence sought to impart to her own characters:

> Ekwensi portrays her in all her often-contradictory moods. She is sharp-witted and calculating, but totally without knowledge of cause and effect, able to bring off small triumphs splendidly, but never able to sort out her own life. She has a temper like red pepper, but she is capable of great affection. She can screech and claw like a she-eagle one moment, and the next moment be as generous with her money and herself as though her whole future were assured. She is tough, enduring, and completely without self-pity. She accepts the world as she finds it, seeing its meanness with an undeceived eye and enjoying its pleasures whenever she can. As a fictional character she will remain alive for a long time. (*LDC*, pp. 156–57)

Few of Laurence's characters are so explosive; they are, after all, Canadian. But they too are unique in their contradictoriness: in the special amalgam of competing impulses that compose their temperaments. Like Jagua, they come to life through the interplay of instinct, reason, and emotion, of knowledge and ignorance, of strength and weakness. They seek clarity of vision, pleasure, and joy in a world that often seems mean and deceitful. They suffer, but they endure.

The vivacity of Africa first inspired Laurence to write because she found there a world of harsh contrasts in which all human faculties are brought into dramatic play. As noted above, Africa gave her the themes of freedom, survival, colonialism, and the plight of women; but it also displayed, in explicit or literal terms, the narrative forms that she would later express psychologically and symbolically. More specifically, it taught her how character, voice, time, and place — the fundamentals of fiction — can be rendered in a consistent artistic vision.

For a first novel, *This Side Jordan* shows remarkable skill and daring. Laurence later felt it was naïvely optimistic, but her enthusiasm encouraged her to experiment with forms she would later refine. Set in Ghana shortly before independence, it interweaves a series of encounters between Africans and British, as well as between ancient, ageless Africa, colonial Africa, and liberated, modern Africa. These encounters are all shocking because the novel is about birth pangs: the trauma preceding and promoting both personal and social liberation. Appropriately, if conveniently, it ends with the birth of two babies, one black and one white. Whether the British are intolerant and rapacious like Johnnie Kestoe or well-meaning like his wife Miranda, they can only aggravate African problems because, as colonizers, they are the problem. The best they can do is mend their own marriage. All the conflicts focus on the young African teacher, Nathaniel Amegbe, who hopes to advance his nation by studying its history and training its young. He is torn between the traditional Africa of the countryside and the new Africa of the city; he is tormented by the inaccessible consolations of the past and the false promises of the future. The more he gets entangled with the Kestoes, the more he inadvertently betrays himself and ruins his prospects. He is trapped "between yesterday and today"[33] until his final, redeeming vision.

This Side Jordan and the short stories in *The Tomorrow-Tamer*, which present the same dilemmas in various moods — tragic, comic, wistful, hopeful, despairing — allowed Laurence to explore a series of related themes and techniques. Most striking is her treatment of the voices of the past, which speak about time, place, ancestry, duty, and the illusions of freedom. Both books resound with the clamour of remembered voices, which give conflicting information, encouragement, and reproach. Characters are haunted by them and must assess, reject, or act upon their advice. It is an advantage of the African setting that these are literally ancestral voices. In "The Voices of Adamo" (*TT*, pp. 205–24), a parable of the fate of Africa, the young Adamo is guided first by "the soft slow woman voice, the voices of gods and grandsires" and then by the word of military command in the army; but when he is discharged and given his lonely freedom, he hears nothing: "Only his own voice which had strangely lost the power of sound, his silent voice splitting his lungs with its cry" (*TT*, pp. 218, 222). Like Africa, Adamo can no longer hear the traditional guidance of the past, nor can he make intelligible the desperate silence of the present. *This Side Jordan* presents a similar dilemma for Nathaniel, who is trapped between a lost but vocal past and a noisy present. He too needs the advice of voices, because "he did not have the gift of spoken words – only of imagined words, when he made silent speeches to himself" (*TSJ*, p. 22). The voices that argue in his mind speak for different times: ancient proverbs compete with modern slogans; tribal drums, with highlife songs; old spells and prophecies, with new, political promises; native languages (Ga, Twi, Fante), with the English taught at the "Futura Academy." Worst of all is the voice of betrayal, repeating

> the words over and over, buzzing in his head like the shrill of a thousand cicadas.
>
> – You have forgotten your own land. You live in the city of strangers, and your god is the god of strangers, and strange speech is in your mouth, and you have no home.
>
> – Oh, Nathaniel, how can a man forget? A man cannot forget. Deep, deep, there lies the image of what the eye has lost and the brain has lost to ready command.
>
> – The forest grows in me, now, this year and the next, until I die. The forest grows in me. (*TSJ*, p. 104)

In a series of lyrical passages like this, Laurence presents the voices of the past, which accuse Nathaniel and lament his treachery to them. They are really the voices of self-accusation and self-betrayal, because Nathaniel, who is educated and more sophisticated than Adamo, no longer believes in the old gods, though he still feels their strange power within him. Laurence had second thoughts about his ornate, poetic voices, pruned them when revising her manuscript, and adopted a more restrained style. But Nathaniel's inner rhapsodies are forerunners of all the monologues, dreams, and debates found in her later novels, and they illustrate her early effort to find an appropriate style, voice, and perspective for the past.

Nathaniel's voices also reveal that the past is deeper and broader than individual memory. Receding in time, the personal past merges with family and tribal pasts, and eventually with a timeless, mythical past. First there is a family past, "a kind of memory-heritage" consisting of "the inherited time of perhaps two or even three past generations, in terms of parents' and grandparents' recollections."[34] The family is a powerful, subtle, coercive force throughout Laurence's work, one which sets standards and examples which seem to be lost yet proclaim themselves in the blood. When Miranda asks Nathaniel to show her some native superstitions, he tries unsuccessfully to disown them, only to discover that they own him: "— What can I say? That this is my heritage? The heritage of Africa, the glorious past" (*TSJ*, p. 158). Through this heritage, he is drawn back to his tribal past. Laurence's fascination with tribalism was encouraged by her years in Africa, which taught her historical and psychological patterns that she then recognized in all social groups, whether Hausa, Ibo, Scots Presbyterian, or Daughters of the American Revolution. She has also acknowledged the influence of O. Mannoni's study *Prospero and Caliban: The Psychology of Colonization.*[35] She appeals to it in a review of Ralph Allen's *Ask the Name of the Lion*, where she describes the tribal personality as follows:

> Tribal man never stands alone. He is guided from his earliest childhood by the tribal customs and by the tribal elders, who in turn are guided by what they consider to be the voices of the ancestors. Past, present and future are thus seen as a continuum. The individual has little or no sense of his separate identity, and cannot even contemplate a life apart from the tribe. He depends for his sense of security on the observance of rituals and on the essentially magical or spiritual power of protectors, the elders and chief, the ancestors and the gods.[36]

Although she refers to African tribes, this description illuminates her Canadian fiction as well, though the emphasis shifts accordingly. Nathaniel and Adamo, as well as Kofi (who helps build a modern bridge, which he then worships) and Godman Pira (who is released from slavery into fearful freedom, something like Adamo), all suffer from being tribal people thrust into a modern world. They must assert themselves as free, responsible individuals in the face of tribal forces which absorb individuality. In order to contemplate a life apart from the tribe, they must release themselves into solitude. To do so is especially painful for Africans because it requires that they — at least at first — betray the past, abjure its magic, and reject its spiritual guidance. In Laurence's terms, they must leave the protection of home before they can return to it and reaffirm their roots, ancestors, and gods.

In the African fiction, these issues are political and social as well as personal because the prevailing colonial conditions charge everyday actions with historical significance. In "A Gourdful of Glory" (*TT*, pp. 225–44), Mammii Ama feels that even riding a bus or selling her bowls will be glorious in a free Ghana, and in a sense she is right. People like Adamo, Kofi, Kwabena, and Ruth Quansah (the last two torn between two cultures) embody the fate of Africa. In *This Side Jordan*, characters are sometimes too obviously social types: the imperialist, the liberal, the traditional or Europeanized African. Consequently, their private lives mirror history: personal freedom corresponds to political independence; debts to the ancestral past express cultural history; the loss of innocence represents Africa entering the post-colonial period. When Johnny Kestoe rapes a young village woman, he repeats the attack on Africa by European imperialism. When, at the end of the novel, Nathaniel exhorts his newborn son, Joshua, to cross the Jordan, he speaks for his homeland.

Rebelling against the present (colonialism) and rejecting the past (tribalism) are painful but necessary in order to assert individual freedom. But the final, paradoxical revelation of Laurence's African writing is that any desire to escape the constraints of time is self-defeating, and any assertion of freedom must take into account human frailty. Freedom from the past is no freedom at all, because to deny the continuity of time is to deny oneself as the product of ancestral and tribal forces. When Nathaniel rejects his gods, he undermines himself. As the tale "Godman's Master" (*TT*, pp. 134–60) illustrates, true freedom entails accepting one's past, one's nature, one's dependence on and responsibility for others; and it entails accepting the insurmountable power of necessity. This will be the great theme of all the Manawaka novels. In *This Side*

Jordan, Nathaniel frees himself only when he recognizes his own powerlessness. Only then does he receive an unexpected gift from the past he had rejected. He is granted what Laurence will later call "grace." In his bewilderment, Nathaniel despairs that man lives in a state of confusion he is powerless to resolve. There is no grace available to him: "A man is better off to have no gods. They're all the same. They take, take, but they never give" (*TSJ*, p. 69). However, he receives help when he needs it most and expects it least. His employer, who has always respected him, offers a better job, and his wife gives him a child, Joshua, whose name suggests hope for the future: "What if things had gone wrong once? They need not again. Now he would have power here, power to change things. And he would change, himself . . . . Nathaniel felt hope flowing back into him" (*TSJ*, pp. 272–73).

After the disputing voices of Africa, Laurence heard only one. It was the voice of Hagar Shipley that prompted the Manawaka novels, each of which records a distinctive pattern of speech, tone, rhythm, allusion, and even slang. Minor characters too are distinguished by their voices, and their relation to the heroine is often given by their contrasting tones. For example, Hagar's reticence is countered and eased by the chirpy conversation of Elva Jardine, a woman who appears only briefly, yet who is wonderfully alive. Laurence has remarked several times that her Canadian novels arose when characters announced themselves and demanded to be heard: "I always start with the main character or, as it may be, characters. Usually there are a number of people who have been inhabiting my head for a number of years before I begin on a novel, and their dilemmas grow out of what they are, where they come from."[37] As we have seen, she calls this the Method novel. Personality comes first; story and details emerge from it; theme and more abstract concerns come later, even after the work is well under way. Most important, characters announce themselves in distinctive voices. If they are compelling individuals who step from the page, it is through their intense, verbal vitality. They live through speech. We "listen to them being themselves"; their ". . . words are not bound by their printed form, for they can be heard"; a good novelist "never makes his characters speak; he listens to them" (*LDC*, pp. 51, 190, 123).

I suggested that Laurence has a good eye for vivid, significant detail. She has a good ear as well and a strong aural imagination, one that responds sensitively to sounds. If fundamentally the novel *is* character for Laurence, and character is registered in speech, then the notion of literary voice — or idiom, as she calls it — is also a fundamental one. It pervades her work and involves much more than dialogue. All the Manawaka books are monologues, either spoken by their heroines in the first person or narrated in a style that imitates their voices. Therefore any comment, no matter how trivial, expresses the presiding personality and leads the reader to the human heart of the novel. In fact, characters speak to themselves as much as to others: their private selves are revealed in the voices that they carefully suppress. One of the delights of *The Stone Angel* is the way Hagar reveals so much more than she says. She has to recognize her own duplicity.

Duplicity, concealment, and dual vision are built into the novel's very form. The ninety-year-old Hagar tells two stories at once, though they are really two aspects of the same story — her life. In the fictional present, she runs away from her son and daughter-in-law after they try to deposit her in the Silverthreads Nursing Home. This is her last rebellion in a long, rebellious life. She escapes to an old cannery, where she has a confessional conversation with a stranger, Murray F. Lees. Then she is taken to a hospital, where she makes two friends before she dies. Interwoven with this simple story are Hagar's memories of her life and of her strained relations with men: her strict, Scottish father; her uncouth but affectionate husband, Bram; her unruly son John. All have died, and she has survived in her loneliness to wander a wilderness of pride, like her biblical namesake (Genesis xvi and xxi). Through the regular alternation of past and present — too regular and chronological, Laurence later felt — we see contrasted the impetuous girl and the wilful old woman. We also get our first view of Manawaka, its tight social hierarchy, its legacy of stubborn strength and scorn for weakness, its reverence for ancestry as represented by Scottish tartans and war cries. Through a clever orchestration of times, Laurence fuses the two story lines so that when, after much self-deception, Hagar finally confesses her sins and asks pardon, she speaks to Murray Lees though she believes it is John. Out of kindness, Lees accepts the role asked of him and grants forgiveness. Later she is reconciled with her other son, Marvin. But Hagar remains proud to the end and never fully accepts that the past is irrevocable. She continues to rage against fate and is admirable for the immense, selfish, unyielding strength that is her undoing. She is, as Marvin says, "a holy terror."[38]

Hagar's speech is so compelling and pervasive that we can see why Laurence claims to prefer *voice* to the vaguer term *style*. This means that all aspects of a novel's language and structure — usually treated as matters of style — derive ultimately from character and its expression in patterns of speech and thought. All depend on the "idiom of narration."[39] Her preference for first-person narrators is logical then because they are the easiest way of suffusing a novel with personality. They provide a dominant voice that sounds in every word and determines the very form of the work. When describing how she writes, Laurence explains that she begins with a character and a voice and then seeks, or simply recognizes, an appropriate form: "I am concerned mainly, I think, with finding a form which will enable a novel to reveal itself, a form through which the characters can breathe."[40] They breathe, live, and talk in their own idiom, and the form or pattern that their narratives take is really the shape or disposition of their minds. Hagar's sequence of flashbacks (like Rachel's debates, Stacey's montage of fantasies, fears, and rebukes, and Morag's "Memorybank Movies") provides recurring structural units expressing the drift of her mind as she assesses her life. To assess one's life, however, means to give it a logical pattern or meaning. For Laurence this means to discover its emotional, intellectual, and moral order. Therefore the orders of story, mind, and life are all the same, and all are governed by voice. To the ancient Hagar, the shape of her whole life simply is a series of disparate memories which she seeks to connect.

Emotional order is the most basic. Hagar tries to make sense of the emotional currents of her life, but she is so volatile that she destroys her own peace of mind. At the time, she turned the men she loved against her, and even in retrospect she challenges and disputes their memory. She illustrates the Black Celt temperament, which feels that we live precariously on the brink of a precipice; she keeps her life tottering. In contrast, it is useful to recall the emotional balance which Laurence found in Africa. In *A Tree for Poverty*, she describes the paradoxical fusion of traits in the Somali character that is so confusing to foreigners. As portrayed in their literature, Somalis freely display both cruelty and kindness, avarice and generosity, duplicity and honesty, simplicity and shrewdness; they revere and scorn poverty; they admire the beautiful and the grotesque. This potent mixture makes life volatile, but far from being destructive, life is remarkably stable, perhaps because the very indulgence of its extremes produces an equilibrium. That stability, rooted in Somali culture and the submissiveness of Islam, sustains the Somalis in a hostile, almost unbearable environment. These qualities recall Ekwensi's character Jagua, whom Laurence admires because her energetic, contradictory impulses are not confounded but balanced, so that she can accept her life even though she is not content with its hardships and injustice. She cannot sort out her life, but can remain more or less at peace amid its commotion. She is as strong as a she-eagle and from her position of strength can be kind, generous, and affectionate as well as fierce. Hagar lacks, or forbids herself, Jagua's tender side because she regards all yielding as a mark of weakness. As a result, she denies herself the emotional stability which she simply calls "joy" and which she associates with music, hymns, and, to some extent, natural beauty. After hearing the minister sing "Come ye before Him and rejoice," she realizes: "I must always, always, have wanted that — simply to rejoice. How is it I never could? . . . Every good joy I might have held, in my man or any child of mine or even the plain light of morning, of walking the earth, all were forced to a standstill by some brake of proper appearances — oh, proper to whom?" (p. 292).

By telling her story, Hagar seeks both joy and propriety. That is, she demands a rational and moral, as well as emotional, order to her life. She has a stern ethical sense, fruit of her Presbyterian upbringing, which insists that cause and effect can be calculated, responsibility can be assessed, blame must be assigned. She reviews her life in order to pronounce a verdict on it. She seeks justice. She reveals this desire to the reader, if not to herself, when at the cannery she fancifully constructs a courtroom from her natural surroundings; she concludes: "Now we need only summon the sparrows as jurors, but they'd condemn me quick as a wink, no doubt"(p. 192). In effect, Hagar puts herself on trial and argues for both prosecution and defence. Even a guilty verdict would be welcome because it would resolve the chaos of her experience into an ethical pattern. Unfortunately, she finds it impossible to assign responsibility or guilt. The chain of effects and causes extends into the past without limit; innumerable factors contributed to any one event. Reversing the perspective, the consequences of her actions were also incalculable; harmless or well-intentioned deeds had terrible but unforeseen results, depriving her first of her husband, then of her son. Murray Lees inadvertently prompts her to exonerate herself when he tries to account for the fire that killed his son while he and his wife were at a revival meeting:

> "I can't figure out whose fault it could have been," he says. "My granddad's, for being a Bible puncher in the first place? Mother's, for making me prefer hellfire to lavender talcum? Lou's, for insisting nothing could happen to him? Mine, for not saying right out, long before, that I might as well not go, for all the good it was doing me?"
>
> Why does he go on like this? I've heard enough. "No one's to blame." (p. 234)

The last words are Hagar's, but she has not yet applied them to her own case. Later when she does, she is still not satisfied, because she has a fierce thirst for justice that life cannot satisfy. She cannot calculate causality, responsibility, propriety, or guilt, but she cannot live without them:

> It's no one's fault, the soft disgusting egg, the shrunken world, the voices that wail like mourners through the night. Why is it always so hard to find the proper one to blame? Why do I always want to find the one? As though it really helped. (p. 264)

Even when justice eludes her, even when she has grounds to acquit herself, Hagar persists in feeling guilty. Like all Laurence's heroines, she has inherited the Presbyterian mentality that makes people "feel guilty at the drop of a hat" and "reproach themselves for the slightest thing" (Cameron, p. 100). Hagar's self-reproach is not slight: "Oh, my two, my dead. Dead by your own hands or by mine?" (p. 292). She exaggerates here, but she also testifies to that powerful moral sense which makes her demand justice, which forces her to condemn herself, and which makes her worthy of pardon. Guilt arises inevitably from feeling responsible for a past that we keep alive in memory but are powerless to change or redeem. "Dead by your own hands or by mine?" she laments, "Nothing can take away those years." It is only when she accepts her powerlessness — a difficult penance for her proud spirit — that she, like Nathaniel, can be redeemed. Like him, she is touched by grace, an unexpected gift which is more human than divine in nature, but which illuminates her life and makes it bearable. She too has rejected her childhood religion but remained haunted by its voices, music, and poetry. She expects only jests, not gifts, from God and assumes there is "no mercy in heaven" (p. 250). For her, grace resides in the fall, not of a sparrow, but of a seagull that she wounds while at the cannery, an accident that brings her the companionship of Murray Lees. She shares her grief with him and finds the forgiveness that, inflexibly, she could never grant herself. Although she cannot find the justice or joy that she needs to bind her long life together, she can reconcile herself to her fate by giving and receiving pardon. Forgiveness does not sort out the confusion of experience, but it accepts that confusion as part of the human lot; it permits concurrence with others and with life. In subsequent scenes, therefore, Hagar pardons, and is pardoned by, a series of characters. But at the very end, she reasserts her pride and refuses to beg for God's pardon or to pray for divine grace. She cannot accept that posture of weakness: "Ought I to appeal? It's the done thing. *Our Father* — no. I want no part of that. All I can think is — *Bless me or not, Lord, just as You please, for I'll not beg*" (p. 307).

Rachel Cameron in *A Jest of God* has no trouble humbling herself or asking forgiveness. The impulse to apologize is instinctive to her, even when faced with strangers: "If I went in there now, unbidden, young to them, strange in my white raincoat, and said *Forgive me*, they would think I had lost my mind."[41] *A Jest of God* is in many ways the reverse of *The Stone Angel*. Rachel is younger (thirty-four years old), has not left Manawaka, has never rebelled against her family or background. She lives in a female world and has not, like Hagar, defined herself through opposition to men. Her father is dead. She is dominated by a possessive, manipulative mother. She is contrasted by her friend, Calla Mackie, whose exuberance is evident in her dress, her speech, her religious enthusiasm, and finally in her lesbianism. Rachel is timid, passive, self-effacing, diffident — all that Hagar despises. She has never fully grown up, and the story is about her maturing. The novel is limited to only one summer (though there are memories stretching into the past) when a crisis forces her to act. She has a love affair with a former acquaintance, Nick Kazlik, and faces the possibility that she is pregnant. An odd joke, a jest of God, is being played on her. It is ironic that so timid and chaste a woman should find herself in this state. In view of her character, her family, her town, it is a catastrophe. It is doubly ironic that she is not really pregnant but has a benign tumour. Although she could lapse back safely into her former life, the crisis forces her to face her sexual and maternal desires, to assert her authority, to accept her independence from, yet connection with, the past: "She tries to break the handcuffs of her own past, but she is self-perceptive enough to recognize that for her no freedom from the shackledom of the ancestors can be total. Her emergence from the tomb-like atmosphere of her extended childhood is a partial defeat — or, looked at in another way, a partial victory" ("Ten Years' Sentences," p. 21). In her own way, she has reached the same conclusion as Nathaniel and Hagar. Unlike Nathaniel, Rachel does not have a baby to lead her into the future, though she longs for one. However, at the end when she takes her mother away from Manawaka, their roles are reversed: her mother is like an elderly child, and Rachel declares herself to be the mother.

The soft-spoken Rachel has to find her own assertive voice, and *A Jest of God* is another novel in which voice, hidden voices, and the voices of the past play an important role. A colloquial tone dominates the book through Rachel's narrative, her monologues, and the debates she conducts with herself as opposing desires and fears dispute each other: "What are you worried about, Rachel? I'm not worried. I'm perfectly all right. Well, relax, then. I am relaxed. Oh? Shut up. Just shut up" (p. 71). In dialogue and in Mrs. Cameron's speeches especially, Laurence very skilfully suggests the complex relationships between people who have known each other all their lives:

> "Well, it's quite all right, dear. I'm only saying if you had let me know, it would've been better, that's all. I could have invited one of the girls in, maybe. Well, never mind. I shall be quite fine here by myself. I'll just slip into my housecoat, and make some coffee, and have a nice quiet evening. I'll be just dandy. Don't you worry about me a speck. I'll be perfectly all right. If you'd just reach down my pills for me from the medicine cabinet. As long as they're where I can get them handily, in case anything happens. I'm sure I'll be fine. You go ahead and enjoy yourself, Rachel." (p. 66)

Mrs. Cameron manipulates her daughter by acting pathetic, yet she is only half aware of her own deception, which, moreover, masks a real dependence on Rachel that Mrs. Cameron only half admits. This tangled situation and the guilt that is Rachel's inevitable response to it are conveyed through the voice with its suppressed irritation, false bravado, and whining. No authorial analysis could accomplish so much so effectively and economically.

Voice has symbolic significance in the novel as well. An elaborate network of references to barbaric speech, spells, prayers, prophecies, holy words, ecstatic utterance, and the gift of tongues expresses Rachel's need to declare herself and to communicate with others. Words have a magical power: they are terrible, passionate, or wonderful; they reveal hidden truths and mysteries so deep that they require a mystic language to give them voice — "the tongues of angels" (p. 27). Rachel's greatest horror is to speak out involuntarily and reveal herself. She lives concealed in silence. For this very reason, she is fascinated with words and plays with them nervously as if to suppress their powers of revelation:

> She said I must see how impossible it would be for her. Yes, I saw, I see. Seesaw. From pillar to post. (p. 12)
>
> "Well — I'll give you a ring, Calla."
>
> What a stupid way of saying you'll phone anyone. There's an ambiguity about the phrase that seems both silly and sinister. I won't say that again. (p. 77)

Rachel associates words with all that is hidden, true, and shameful. She imagines her baby as a voice crying within her. She discovers that in love ". . . one speaks from faith, not logic . . ."(p. 148). She echoes the Rachel of the Bible: once when demanding a child from Nick, revealing a desire she had not recognized in herself (Genesis xxx); again when mourning the loss of what she thought was her baby (Jeremiah xxxi). Most revealing of all is a superbly shocking scene when she accompanies Calla to the "Tabernacle of the Risen and Reborn." She finds to her horror that she is the one blessed, or cursed, with the gift of tongues. The desire, despair, and grief suppressed in her find their own terrible voice. The tension of her self-restraint is released:

> Silence. I can't stay. I can't stand it. I really can't. Beside me, the man moans gently, moans and stirs, and moans —

> *That voice!*
>
> Chattering, crying, ululating, the forbidden transformed cryptically to nonsense, dragged from the crypt, stolen and shouted, the shuddering of it, the fear, the breaking, the release, the grieving –
>
> Not Calla's voice. Mine. Oh my God. Mine. The voice of Rachel. (p. 36)

The voice within her also arises from more remote sources. Her personal past is not as long and vocal as Hagar's, but she has an ancestry corresponding to the tribal past of the African fiction. Tribal man, as we have seen, never stands alone because he lives in a continuum of past, present, and future, a continuum marked by ancestral voices which challenge a character's individuality. Rachel, like all Laurence's Canadian heroines who are modern, Western individualists, wishes to stand alone but cannot do so confidently or without guilt because she feels intimidated by ancestral voices. She resents their authority. It is true, as critics have insisted, that there is a powerful sense of solitude in Laurence's novels, especially *A Jest of God*, which shows the essential loneliness of the individual due to the unbridgeable gap between people.[42] However, loneliness does not arise from living in anonymity or in a social vacuum. It derives from, and is intensified by, living within an intricate web of family and tribal connections, a network of pressures from the past that fail to offer comfort or guidance. Rachel is Laurence's most timorous and solitary heroine, but she has no doubt of her ancestry: "Half the town is Scots descent and the other half is Ukrainian . . . . the Scots knew how to be almightier than anyone but God. She [Mrs. Cameron] was brought up that way, and my father too, and I, but by the time it reached me, the backbone had been splintered considerably" (p. 65). Rachel feels feeble and alone in the face of her strong heritage. She feels manipulated by ancestral voices which have become instinctive, but which she tries to resist. For example, at one point she finds herself being condescending to Nick:

> Whatever he thinks, it's not even approaching the truth. Who does he think he is? High School or not. Nestor Kazlik's son. The milkman's son.
>
> It can't be myself thinking like that. I don't believe that way

> at all. It's as though I've thought in Mother's voice. Nick graduated from university. I didn't. (p. 64)

In his own way, Nick faces the same problem. He is ambivalent about his Ukrainian heritage; he both resents and admires his father; he feels a threat to his identity, as he shows by alluding to his dead, twin brother:

> "I used to be glad we weren't the same, that's all. How would you like there to be someone exactly the same as yourself?"
>
> I've never thought about it. Would it make a person feel more real or less so? Would there be some constant communication, with no doubt about knowing each other's meanings, as though your selves were invisibly joined? (p. 84)

Rachel's questions point to the central issues of the novel. How can a person feel "real" or authentic when she is divided within and against herself, when she speaks in conflicting voices, when she resents the family roots which support her, when she cannot communicate with those to whom she is most intimately joined? Her desire for, yet fear of, true intimacy – "constant communication" – shows that for Laurence the notion of voice implies the whole intricate, painful enterprise of personal and literary communication. When Rachel says, though only to herself, "*Nick – listen*" (p. 154), she is calling for the attention of a sympathetic audience. Hagar, in *The Stone Angel*, made the same silent appeal: "*Listen. You must listen. It's important*" (p. 282). In an essay appropriately entitled "Listen. Just Listen," Laurence treats the need for communication between French and English Canada in the same way: "If we are to listen truly to what they are saying, we must take into ourselves views which are passionate, though passionately different from our own, views which extend beyond our experience but which also encompass our history."[43] All of these calls spring from the hope that a listener, simply by listening, can offer understanding, comfort, and absolution. They are also the storyteller's appeal for an audience, echoing the voice of the Ancient Mariner, whom Hagar and Morag mention, compelling the listener to share his tale and ease his burden. Laurence became sensitive to this appeal in Africa, which provoked, yet defied, her desire to hear the voices and see with the eyes of Somali tribesmen. In the novels of Chinua Achebe especially, she found her own literary task:

> He shows the impossibly complicated difficulties of one person speaking to another, attempting to make himself known to another, attempting to hear — really to hear — what another is saying. In his novels, we see man as a creature whose means of communication are both infinitely subtle and infinitely clumsy, a prey to invariable misunderstandings. Yet Achebe's writing also conveys the feeling that we must attempt to communicate, however imperfectly, if we are not to succumb to despair or madness. The words which are spoken are rarely the words which are heard, but we must go on speaking. (*LDC*, pp. 124–25)

These remarks remain valid if we substitute Laurence's name for Achebe's.

The dilemmas of personal identity — knowledge and assurance of oneself — and of communication as the fragile but precious means of confirming identity both continue in *The Fire-Dwellers*. They are elaborated in a novel which is broader, busier, funnier, and more aggravated than *A Jest of God*. These qualities reflect the personality of Stacey MacAindra. She is Rachel's thirty-nine-year-old sister, who has moved from Manawaka to Vancouver, where she struggles with four children and an overworked husband who faces a crisis in his career. She is upset, not only by personal and family problems, but by social unrest, by her fear that she lives in the midst of a disastrous world that violently consumes itself in the extremes of war or feverish prosperity. This is Laurence's first attempt to restore to her novels the social scope of her African writing. She does not discuss historical and social issues, as she will in *The Diviners*; instead, she presents Stacey's confused awareness of them as she watches television, reads newspapers, and observes the youth of Vancouver in the 1960s. Advertisements, the Vietnamese war (not named), crime, drugs, and nuclear weapons all contribute to her sense of catastrophe. She is a fire-dweller trapped in the flames of modern society.

Her confusion is expressed, once again, as an aspect of voice and time — the voices of past and present. The novel records either a babble of conflicting voices or a painful silence. On one hand, she complains: "I'm surrounded by voices all the time but none of them seem to be saying anything, including mine."[44] On the other, she is afraid, or unable, to speak. Several characters have embarrassing, secret names (Clifford, Arbuckle, Anastasia, Vernon Winkler), suggesting hidden, silent selves. Stacey's youngest child, Jen, has never spoken, as if "determined not to communicate," though Stacey tries to teach her "a few human words" (pp. 5, 3). Stacey and her husband, Mac, cannot communicate their fears, and their conversations grow absurdly inconsequential:

> Stacey, everything is okay. How many times do I have to say it? Can't you please for heaven's sake quit yakking about my work?
> I'm sorry. But you won't talk. You won't ever say.
> There is nothing to say.
> Oh well in that case
> Look, what do you *want* me to say?
> I don't *want* you to say anything
> Then why do you keep on
> I'm sorry it's just that (p. 79)

Laurence uses fragments, spacing, italics, and indenting to fuse and confuse a parade of voices, memories, dreams, songs, thoughts, and conversations. She temporarily obscures the difference between what is said aloud and what is thought. The effect is sometimes comical:

> Now, I don't want any of you girls to feel you have to, but if you'd like to look at the various pieces of Polyglam
> These sandwich cases are just perfectly
> What adorable eggcups
> It's this cookie jar that I think is so
> — If I get out of here for less than ten bucks it will be a bloody miracle. (pp. 86–87)

Stacey's tone and style are unmistakable. More seriously, this play of voices, real and imagined, expresses her growing confusion and loss of control, and it reveals the anarchic impulse in her that is both playful and dangerous. The abrupt intrusion of her inner voice demonstrates her need to escape into memory and reverie, to review her life for clues to her present dilemma. It makes her a rich, complex character.

The voices from her past announce both the disjunction and continuity of time. Stacey frequently complains that she is adrift in an aimless, eddying present, yet vivid memories link her to a past that seems at once remote and omnipresent. The past, and with it her youth, plans, and hopes, is irrevocably gone, leaving her older, sadder, and heavier; yet it persists like Nathaniel's gods with a strange power that threatens the present. It speaks with the voice of reproach about betrayal and loss, but because it is past, there is no way to confront it. Like so many of Laurence's characters, Stacey wrestles with ghosts that are powerful yet insubstantial. She feels branded by stigmata because she cannot bake bread, because she drinks and eats too much, because she worries over trifles. She has a genius for self-recrimination and, as she surveys her life, traces the chain of guilt right back to Original Sin: "Where did it start? Everything goes too far back to be traced. The roots vanish, because they don't end with Matthew, even if it were possible to trace them that far. They go back and back forever. Our father Adam" (p. 167). Stacey's self-reproach demonstrates that she too is a product of the Presbyterian upbringing she has rejected. Through her conversations with God, through her "sense of some monstrous injustice" (p. 12), she shows that, like Hagar, she wishes to find a just and joyful meaning to her life. That she is not merely obsessed with her own petty discomfort but is moral and serious becomes clear when she meets an old Manawaka acquaintance, Valentine Tonnerre, a Métis whose sister had been burned to death. Stacey hears the voice of another fire-dweller and condemns herself for personal, social, and historical wrongs:

> Even her [Valentine's] presence is a reproach to me, for all I've got now and have been given and still manage to bitch on and on about it. And a reproach for the sins of my fathers, maybe. The debts are inherited and how could the damage ever be undone or forgiven? I don't want to, but I seem to believe in a day of judgment, just like all my Presbyterian forebears did, only I don't think it'll happen in the clouds or elsewhere and I don't think I'll be judged for the same things they thought they'd be. (p. 265)

How could the damage ever be undone or forgiven? This was Hagar's question as well: her undoing could only be answered by forgiveness. Both women respond by trying to *compose* their lives in two senses. They seek to establish the patterns that give their lives meaning, and they seek to narrate them. "I would sort out and understand my life . . . ," Stacey says (p. 172). The two tasks, understanding and narrating (or giving voice to), are really the same. Stacey's first effort, however, is a kind of recomposition. She tries to remake herself in order to fit into society. She dresses appropriately, buys plastic kitchenware, and plays the role of a businessman's elegant wife. This fiasco permits Laurence to satirize modern commercialism, female fashions, and the middle-class dream of the good life ("Richalife"), which depends more on insecurity and fear of death than on any secure sense of value. A secure sense of value is precisely what Stacey needs but what her experience seems to refute. At the other extreme is the example set by Mac's friend Buckle Fennick. He presents himself as a swaggering, sensual individual who refuses to submit to social pressure as he drives his giant truck ferociously across British Columbia. In contrast to Stacey, his identity seems secure because he asserts it through the force of his desires and his will. Theo Q. Dombrowski discusses the importance of willpower in Laurence's work, noting that her protagonists display a "sensibility caught between its own inner authority and the more brutal authority of the world without." Depending on the opposing forces, characters are either wilful (Hagar) or will-less (Rachel) and must learn how to exert their will or how to recognize its limitations and submit to facts.[45] Stacey does both, but only after she sees in Buckle the perverse, tormenting illusions that will can fabricate. Buckle proves to be the reverse of what he seems. His life is a poorly composed fiction. Unable to accept his suppressed homosexuality, he becomes increasingly superstitious, obscene, and finally suicidal. Like Calla in *A Jest of God*, he presents in sexual terms a form of self-assertion and self-denial that the heroine cannot adopt.

Instead, Stacey sorts out her life in the same two ways as all Laurence's protagonists — through action and through contemplation. Although both prove ambiguous, they provide at least a provisional means of self-discovery. Action is the simpler. While the actions taken in Laurence's novels sometimes seem slight, they are still important psychologically and symbolically as self-assertive deeds: characters take their lives into their own hands. Hagar runs away. Rachel has a love affair. Stacey too has an affair with a young man she hardly knows and who therefore can act as confessor and confidant. Hagar found a similar figure in Murray Lees. In each case, the stranger, because he is removed from family and tribal entanglements, offers both the intimacy and the impersonality that the heroine needs. He offers shelter and escape. Nick is Ukrainian. Jules Tonnerre in *The Diviners* is Métis. Luke Venturi in *The Fire-Dwellers* is Italian. He lives outside Vancouver in a peaceful, natural setting where Stacey hears no voices except the cry of birds. He provides a touch of extravagance, of psychological and sexual release, which the impulsive strain in her requires. Temporarily she escapes into romance and dreams of a further escape into the primitive wilds of British Columbia, suitably evoked in a series of lyrical descriptions. This was Buckle's territory too, but unlike him, Stacey does not succumb to the illusion that it encourages. There is no escape from self. She is shocked back to reality — however tenuous she then finds it — when she discovers Luke is only twenty-four and therefore she is as old as his mother. Her childish romance merely confirms her age and the truths she was trying to escape.

Contemplation — the effort to observe, understand, and judge herself — is even more difficult for Stacey. Memory is inaccurate or treacherous. Causality and responsibility cannot be assessed. The voices of the past cannot be answered. Guilt cannot be allayed. "Who is this *you*?" (p. 171), Stacey asks herself when she feels baffled by her own identity. The effort to define a stable ego subverts itself by entangling her in illusion, inconsistency, and contradiction. Theo Dombrowski concludes that ". . . the self must remain ultimately enigmatic" for Laurence, and this puzzle is "the ironic answer to the questions she so persistently asks" about identity.[46] Yet in a further paradox, the attempt to define identity is itself a clue to one's true character. The nature of the effort, its sincerity, tenacity, honesty, rigour, and so on, displays to the reader, if not immediately to the individual, the personality at issue. It reveals especially the moral strenuousness of characters who demand justice in their chaotic lives. In *The Fire-Dwellers*, Stacey uses the image of "mental baggage" to express the conditions of her bewilderment and of her ultimate victory. (Laurence repeats the image in her essay "Ten Years' Sentences.") As we advance through life, we carry an ever-increasing load of memories and regrets, which we must occasionally unpack and examine: "Too much mental baggage. Too damn much, at this point. More more more than I want. Things keep spilling out of the suitcases, taking me by surprise, bewildering me as I stand on the platform" (p. 37). Mental baggage suggests that life is a journey through time, that we carry with us the past and its burden of guilt, that the mind is an untidy, overstuffed container. But it also suggests that Stacey is strong enough to carry her bags. Unpacking them means reviewing, analyzing, judging – in short, composing the narrative that forms this novel.

In one of his essays, George Steiner defines identity as "a sustained act of privacy."[47] Seen in this light, Stacey's long, active, strained but sustained contemplation of her life *is* her identity. By telling her story she proves her worth, first to the reader, gradually to herself. The proof, however, remains antiheroic and anticlimactic. At the end, she reluctantly admits: "Now I see that whatever I'm like, I'm pretty well stuck with it for life. Hell of a revelation that turned out to be" (p. 299). There is no joyous revelation such as Nathaniel proclaimed to his new son. There is no room for heroes in *The Fire-Dwellers*, though there will be in *The Diviners*. Magnificent Thor Thorlakson proves to be skinny Vernon Winkler in disguise. There is only the everyday heroism of ordinary people who manage to remain decent in an indecent world. Stacey learns to accept more or less patiently the things that cannot be changed, that defy human will or calculation; and she learns to recognize and use her considerable powers. Her strength of character makes this conclusion bearable because she, like Jagua and all Laurence's characters, is really sustained by a strength which she always possessed but did not know how to exercise. While other people admired her skill and resourcefulness, she felt feeble and inept. Finally she can assert herself in the face of time, loss, age, and death. She cannot fully understand or master reality, but she can live with it: "I can't stand it. I cannot. I can't take it. Yeh, I can, though. By God, I can, if I set my mind to it" (p. 289).

Laurence's next book, *A Bird in the House*, presents the memoirs of Vanessa MacLeod, who recalls her youth in Manawaka. The chapters are discrete stories which were published separately but intended, Laurence insists, as parts of a single work. It is her most autobiographical work: Vanessa explores her family, her surroundings, and her own talents and gradually discovers her vocation as a writer. She looks ahead to a more accomplished writer: Morag Gunn in *The Diviners*. Perhaps Laurence's natural reticence, combined with the episodic structure, explains why *A Bird in the House* is less dense and passionate than her other works and why Vanessa is a less compelling character. However, it presents more modestly all of Laurence's recurring concerns: stern grandparents and their Celtic heritage; family loyalties and rebellion; death; the house, clan, or tribe as a sustaining but intimidating force; love and its complications; the paradoxes of guilt, freedom, and justice; the Canadian West; the dispossessed (for example, the Tonnerre family) who were displaced so that Manawaka could prosper.

A Bird in the House illustrates with special clarity the subtle interdependence of time and voice, which I have treated so far, following the example of *This Side Jordan*, as the "voices of the past." In fact, the relation is more complex than this metaphor suggests. The opening of *A Bird in the House* hints at a dialectic of past and present, an interplay of voices in time: "That house in Manawaka is the one which, more than any other, I carry with me" ("The Sound of the Singing," in *BH*, p. 3). The memories to which Vanessa gives voice are all present; they are part of her mental baggage. But through them she seeks access to a past that speaks dramatically for itself. According to the convention of the confessional novel, the past can be recalled perfectly. It is not just related, but recreated. (Laurence will both honour and subvert this convention in *The Diviners*, where Morag questions the accuracy of her memories.) The past speaks for itself but uses the voice of the present. The mature, narrating Vanessa presides over the book even as she conjures up the texture of her youth. In a commentary on the short story "To Set Our House in Order" (*BH*, pp. 39–59), Laurence explains why she adopted this narrative strategy:

> What I tried to do was definitely *not* to tell the story as though it were being narrated by a child. This would have been impossible for me and also would have meant denying the story one of its dimensions, a time-dimension, the viewing from a distance of events which had happened in childhood. The narrative voice had to be that of an older Vanessa, but at the same time the narration had to be done in such a way that the ten-year-old would be conveyed. The narrative voice, therefore, had to speak as though from two points in time, simultaneously. ("Time and the Narrative Voice," pp. 158–59)

A child's voice and vision would be too limited. Children are too young to have a past and too inarticulate to speak with authority. The story requires a double perspective that combines the freshness of a girl's perception with the maturity of a woman's judgement. The duality of time, the constant interplay of past and present, is thus implicit in the narrative voice. So is the duplicity of time. It gives experience but destroys innocence; it replaces hope with regret; it betrays its promises.

Vanessa reveals the power of time to both heal and hurt when she recalls how she was jilted by her first boyfriend. Her mother can offer only ambiguous comfort:

> ". . . I know you won't believe me, honey, but after a while it won't hurt so much. And yet in a way I guess it always will, to some extent. There doesn't seem to be anything anybody can do about that."
>
> As it happened, she was right on all counts. I did not at the time believe her. But after a while it did not hurt so much. And yet twenty years later it was still with me to some extent, part of the accumulation of happenings which can never entirely be thrown away. ("Jericho's Brick Battlements," in *BH*, pp. 201–02)

This incident combines the pain and disillusionment of the moment with the wisdom and regret of retrospection. It illustrates nicely how the narrative voice can speak from two points in time simultaneously. Most important, it shows how Vanessa's effort to communicate her life-story reveals in the very process of speaking the historical nature of both life and story. First, it displays how her life is conditioned and complicated by the flow of time. Her personality is not static; it evolves, accumulates, and alters with age. The notions of inheritance and survival, which Laurence says are central to all her novels, implicate a character in time, binding her to past and future. David L. Jeffrey argues that Laurence's fascination with time is peculiarly Canadian because it reflects our belief in the existence, utility, and necessity of historical meaning. People cannot understand themselves or their plight in isolation; they need the context of larger cultural forces. When Vanessa complains, "I wanted only to be by myself, with no one else around" ("The Sound of the Singing," in *BH*, p. 35), she does not yet realize that even her most solitary concern with personal identity requires that she see her own life as part of something larger and older. In Canadian fiction, Jeffrey explains, the historical perspective is manifested in a concern with the family, which links the individual to a lineage through time and to "a conception of the present as an occasion for inheritance and procreation." Even Hagar, a very private person, can conceive of her life only as a "life-in-family," a series of experiences that she has shared intimately with others.[48] Laurence's characters are, whether they like it or not, essentially historical beings.

Second, Vanessa's effort to tell her story implicates her in time because the novel is itself a temporal art. The progressive telling of a story — narrative — is a temporal process. "Fiction," explains Laurence, ". . . becomes a matter of the individual characters moving within a history which includes past, present and future" ("Ivory Tower or Grassroots?" p. 17). But we have already seen that she regards narrative as essentially a matter of voice. The link between time and voice, the chronology and the idiom of narration, is clarified by her definition of idiom as "the ways of speech and memory" ("Ten Years' Sentences," p. 22). Recollection is a style. A voice is young or old, naïve or experienced, hopeful or regretful. It sounds with inherited inflections, colloquialisms, and cadences that reveal the speaker's past, family, and social background. "'Well, as your grandmother says, there's no use getting in a fantod about it,' my mother said," reports Vanessa ("The Sound of the Singing," in *BH*, p. 15), thereby continuing the family tradition for a third generation. When Laurence's characters speak in the voice of memory, they register the passing of time in their style, and by speaking, they seek to ease the burden of the past. Vanessa's burden is not as heavy as Hagar's or Stacey's, because she is younger and her life has been less catastrophic. However, she too must communicate as both a means of understanding and a ritual of expiation. She must speak in order to make peace with her past. In particular, she must come to terms with her grandfather, Timothy Connor, the patriarchal figure whom she regarded as the domineering villain of the family. Yet in the final story — "Jericho's Brick Battlements" — it is from him and the family past he embodies that she receives a kind of blessing. She has an involuntary memory: ". . . I remembered something I didn't know I knew. I remembered riding in the MacLaughlin-Buick with my grandfather. It was a memory with nothing around it, an unplaced memory without geography or time." She recalls flying triumphantly through Manawaka: "*A-hoo-gah! A-hoo-gah!* I was gazing with love and glory at my giant grandfather as he drove his valiant chariot through all the streets of this world" (*BH*, pp. 178, 179). Later, when he dies, this "memory of a memory" (*BH*, p. 206) returns of its own accord and becomes an emblem of the whole book, which is Vanessa's triumphant tour of her life. Through it she confirms the intensity and the intricacy of her feeling for her family, her past, and especially for her grandfather, whom she had feared and rejected, but whom she finally acknowledges as her ancestor.

The Diviners is Laurence's most elaborate novel and the summation of her career because it unites characters, incidents, symbols, themes, and techniques from all her previous work. By now she knows the world of Manawaka so well that she can roam freely within it. This does not mean it is her best novel, only her most complete and self-conscious. Because Morag Gunn is a perceptive and articulate artist, she discusses openly those problems that the early heroines only sensed. She makes explicit the formal concerns that previously were only implied by the narrative style. For example, unlike Vanessa, she knows that as she reviews her life she is really presenting *"invented memories."*[49] The memory derives from the past, but the invention is in the present. The time scheme is dual. Memory is a creative project through which she composes her past by discovering its significant patterns. She is the director of, as well as actress in, her "Memorybank Movies." She treats herself like a fictional character because she is writing a novel, which she completes at the end and names, presumably, *The Diviners*. Therefore the novel is not only about Morag, but about the processes of memory and imagination: "A daft profession. Wordsmith. Liar, more likely. Weaving fabrications. Yet, with typical ambiguity, convinced that fiction was more true than fact. Or that fact was in fact fiction" (p. 21).

This wordplay illustrates how the novel is sometimes too intent on displaying its own ingenuity. Yet ingenuity — the divinings of the imagination — is its subject, and Morag is vibrant enough as a character to sustain it dramatically. At the age of forty-seven, she is worried about her restless, teenage daughter, Pique, and is struggling to write her novel. She lives in rural Ontario beside a river that, through an effect of the wind, appears to flow both ways. It serves as an emblem of time, recollection, and divination: *"Look ahead into the past, and back into the future, until the silence"* (p. 370). Meanwhile Morag is beset by memories, and the novel, like *The Stone*

Angel, is composed through a counterpoint of past and present. She recalls her uncomfortable childhood in Manawaka, where she was raised by the garbage collector and his wife; her cultured and sheltered life in Toronto as wife of her former English professor; her rebellion and flight to Vancouver and Britain, where she developed as a writer; her return to Canada and her roots; and her lasting love for Jules Tonnerre. Like Hagar, Morag tends to define herself in opposition to men: her surrogate father, Christie Logan; her husband, Brooke Skelton; her lovers, Jules and Dan McRaith; her mentor, Royland the water diviner; her heroic ancestors, Piper Gunn and Rider Tonnerre.

Morag shares with all Laurence's misfits problems of identity, injustice, will, guilt, and betrayal, but she views them in a broader perspective. Through her imaginative sympathy, she sees her own misfortune as a fragment of something much more grand and terrible. She does so, not with Stacey's confused sense of disaster, but with a deeper, more informed insight that discovers a tragic dimension in her story. She is an everyday heroine much like Stacey, but her story reveals heroism of a larger order. Tragedy and heroism were suggested in Laurence's African fiction, but were restrained in her more domestic, Canadian novels. Hagar rejects divine comfort; Rachel does not know she echoes the Bible; Stacey belittles her own courage; Vanessa has only a glimpse of her grandfather as a glorious charioteer. The chariot returns triumphantly in *The Diviners*, where it is driven by legendary figures such as Piper Gunn, Rider Tonnerre, and the Celtic hero, Cuchullin:

> A chariot! the great chariot of war,
> Moving over the plain with death!
> The shapely swift car of Cuchullin,
> True son of Semo of hardy deeds.
>
> (p. 51)

Morag hears this poem when she is a girl, and the words sound magical to her. Later she discovers their power lies in their ability to display images of human excellence and tragedy, beautiful images that illuminate and dignify the everyday world. Behind Jules, his poverty and despair, stands Rider Tonnerre. The settling of the Canadian West and the founding of Manawaka required the dispossession of the Métis, symbolized for Morag by the fire that destroyed the

Tonnerre home. Behind Christie and his bitter self-reproach stands Piper Gunn. He belongs to another tale of dispossession in which the Scots were driven from their homes to Canada by the "Bitch-Duchess" of Sutherland. Dan McRaith's painting of their burning crofts provides Morag with a corresponding symbol. Similarly, Christie's war cry, "The Ridge of Tears," at first seems just another of his colourful oddities; but she gradually realizes that it expresses the pathos of human fate. She feels herself mysteriously caught up in history and fate when she and Jules exchange gifts. He gives her a plaid pin, which had originally belonged to Hagar in *The Stone Angel*; she gives him a knife, marked with the letter *T*, which had belonged to Lazarus Tonnerre. As these items pass back and forth between the Curries, Shipleys, Tonnerres, and Gunns, they stitch together the ancestral pasts in a common fate.

As these items change hands, they become relics offering the blessing of the past. They become signs of the deepest past of all, in which opposing individuals, families, and tribes are reconciled through the ancient stories and places that they share. "Beyond your great-grandparents," Laurence explains, ". . . the ancestors become everybody's ancestors" (Cameron, p. 113). Eventually the long lines of Western Canadian families inhabit a common past which, from the vantage of the present, appears legendary rather than historical. At this point, "their past has misted into myth."[50] The mythical past is history reviewed by the imagination. Just as Morag half recalls and half creates her own past, and the resulting invented memories are true for her, so, through a "collective cultural memory" ("Time and the Narrative Voice," p. 156), do we mythicize history and give it the passionate truth of art. It is a marvellous coincidence that pin and knife should find their way into Morag's and Jules' hands, but the relics are signs of a coincidence and marvel of another kind. The histories of their antagonistic families coincide by exhibiting the same epic pattern, following the parallel lives of Piper Gunn and Rider Tonnerre, both real people transmuted into legendary heroes. Their marvellous tales gain the permanence of art in Morag's novel and Jules' songs. Beyond the rebukes and disputes of time lies a shared, mythical timelessness, which, in all her novels, Laurence invokes through literary and biblical allusions. Myths are timeless in the sense that they are universal, endlessly repeating the human drama of origins, banishment, and homecoming. Her characters' lives are set against, sometimes within, a backdrop of recurring patterns:

myths of ancestry (Genesis), exile (Exodus), judgement and salvation (Revelation). Hagar and Rachel pay no attention to their biblical namesakes; Stacey quotes the Bible and the classics, though only to mock herself; only Morag is literate and imaginative enough to recognize and benefit from her correspondence with myth. She becomes a modern mythmaker by writing about "that giant of a man, Piper Gunn, who probably never lived in so-called real life but who lives forever" (p. 341). By writing, she finds a way of living with the past, in two senses of the phrase. Literature makes the past eternally present: "The myths are my reality" (p. 319), she tells Dan. And it makes the past bearable. By writing, she does not disentangle the web of the past — something all Laurence's characters try but fail to do — so much as trace the intricate patterns of the web, and give them a tragic beauty.

The timelessness of myth also derives from a reverence for place. The past requires a native soil; it endures in sacred locations. In the African stories, ancestral voices speak from the forest and river, which belong to the local gods who make their homes there. The genius, or spirit, of place continues to speak in the Canadian stories, at first quietly and then more assertively in the voices of nature. Rachel questions the spruce trees and autumn leaves for messages. Stacey and Rachel, in *The Fire-Dwellers*, listen to the lunatic voices of the loons: "witch birds out there in the night lake, or voices of dead shamans, mourning the departed Indian gods" (p. 172). Morag moves even closer to a mystical sense of nature. She makes a pilgrimage to Scotland, thinking it is her native land, but realizes her true home is in the Canadian prairie. Meanwhile Laurence has been collecting images of Canada — prairie, trees, Canada geese, Batoche, Galloping Mountain, the geography of Manawaka, the river that flows both ways — images for Morag to claim as her own when she comes home. She returns just in time for Christie's death, and for his burial amid "the sickly over-sweet perfume of peonies but also the clean dry pungency of the tall low-boughed spruces" (p. 328).

Through his suffering, his love for Morag, and his powers as a diviner, he sanctifies the ground. She then can recognize that ". . . the light-leafed willows and tall solid maples were like ancestors, carrying within themselves the land's past"(p. 235). Later she participates in a water-divining, and watches Royland reveal the sources of life within the earth. Laurence herself was able to commune with the spirit of place when she made a pilgrimage to the battlefield of Batoche and heard voices "everywhere in the wind." Although these were Métis voices, they spoke to her, joining her ancestors and theirs to the land they disputed, shared, and sanctified: "But there are more and deeper things between myself and Riel, myself and Dumont. We are prairie." In the deepest past and most attentive present, people, place, and time are fused. Laurence and Morag have almost returned to the mysticism of the African stories, but not quite. The fusion takes place only in the imagination of the sympathetic observer who feels: "We in spirit, being linked to the land, are also linked to the ancestral voices which arise out of many sources."[51]

Morag seeks the blessing of one other mythmaker. She quotes from *The Tempest* and comments: ". . . 'What strength I have's mine own, Which is most faint — ' If only he [Prospero] can hang onto that knowledge, that would be true strength. And the recognition that his real enemy is despair within, and that he stands in need of grace, like everyone else — Shakespeare did know just about everything" (p. 270). Like Rachel and Stacey, she must learn how to wield her will power and how to accept its limitations. However, "grace" is the final term mentioned, as it was in the quotation that began this discussion. There too it was a response to the human individual's paradoxical combination of strength and weakness: the human spirit is "amazingly strong and yet in need of strength and grace." Laurence frequently adopts a religious vocabulary, but we must be careful in seeking eternal solutions to the temporal dilemmas in her stories, in turning from reason and its failure to faith, from justice to divine mercy, from confusion to revelation. Like her characters, she is sceptical of the doctrinal religion in which she was raised, though she continues to admire its spirit, its rituals, and its imagery. Hymns especially appear in all her novels, startling characters who thought they had forgotten them. In interviews, her comments on religion have been cautious. She told Donald Cameron that she was a "kind of religious atheist, if you like, or religious agnostic" who feels that God is not totally dead in our universe (Cameron, p. 111). She reaffirmed this belief to Alan Twigg and added that art is "in some way" religious, not when it preaches, but when it "points to the mystery at the heart of things, the mystery and wonder at the core of every human individual."[52] Thus Adele Wiseman's *Crackpot* is a "profoundly religious work, in the very broadest sense, ultimately a celebration of life and of the mystery which is at the heart of life."[53]

In this sense, she would surely consider herself a religious novelist. She shows that despite, and even because of, their faults, people have something precious in their hearts, a mystery which makes them worthy of pity, love, and reverence. She considers the "mystery at the heart of things" in the Christian terms with which she is familiar, and she is true to her Protestant heritage in stressing grace as a response to our inherent weakness. Grace is "God's unmerited free, spontaneous love for sinful man revealed and made effective in Jesus Christ."[54] It is offered to man, not as a reward for good conduct, but as an abundant gift to save him from his own sinful, helpless failure: "since all have sinned and fall short of the glory of God, they are justified by his grace as a gift, through the redemption which is in Christ Jesus, whom God put forward as an expiation by his blood, to be received by faith" (Romans iii. 23–25). In Laurence's novels, grace is a gift, freely given through pity and love. She compares it to poetic inspiration, which the artist receives mysteriously and then uses carefully, but for which he or she is not ultimately responsible:

> Many writers, including myself, who even though they were not thinking in any specific religious terms, have experienced something while writing which I think of as a kind of grace. This came very naturally to ancient and tribal peoples. They described it as possession by the gods. Nowadays when people say they have written something that surprises them, in my terms there's a sense of grace happening there.[55]

This "gift, or portion of grace" (*The Diviners*, p. 369), makes possible the art of the diviner. However, in her religious agnosticism, Laurence, unlike the good Christian, does not consider grace enough to ensure salvation; nor does she turn for redemption to Christ and His sacrifice. She turns only to men and women and the human community. Diviners, artists, and people generally, cannot expect to be saved by their gifts, only inspired by them. From her early story "The Drummer of All the World" to her last, she has insisted that salvation comes only from within oneself, and one person cannot find it for another: "No one can save anyone else. We can only try to make them aware of our caring."[56] The gift is caring, not salvation, and it is "the stubborn ability of humans to keep on living and caring what happens to others" that redeems them and gives them "a kind of heroic quality."[57]

Kenneth C. Russell pursues this line of thought further. He contends that Laurence has a "profound and theologically sound sense of the mystery of grace," which she displays in a "providential pattern" in the lives of her characters.[58] Ultimately they are guided and blessed by God when they sense some extraordinary, transcendent value that supports them: "Some purpose and meaning graciously sustains their existence and enables them to make an act of trust in life itself."[59] I find it difficult to detect the hand of providence, but I agree that it is in life itself that joy is asserted, and that grace contributes to the pattern of assertion. Grace takes many forms, some apparently trivial, but it is always an unexpected offering of sympathy, forgiveness, or compassion. Often it is a gift from the past, healing the wounds of time and change by giving the continuity that desire, reason, and judgement failed to supply. The plaid pin that mysteriously makes its way into Morag's hands is a good example of an unsolicited, gracious token from the past. When she checks it in her book of clans and tartans, she finds a motto appropriate for her own Clan Gunn; she finds the inspiration she needs: "*My Hope Is Constant In Thee*. It sounds like a voice from the past. Whose voice, though? Does it matter? It does not matter. What matters is that the voice is there, and that she has heard these words which have been given to her" (p. 353). It is hope itself that is given to her. She feels the consecration of her ancestral past and looks ahead with some confidence to the future.

NOTES

[1] Margaret Laurence, Introd., *House of Hate*, by Percy Janes, New Canadian Library, No. 124 (Toronto: McClelland and Stewart, 1976), p. x.

[2] Donald Cameron, "Margaret Laurence: The Black Celt Speaks of Freedom," in *Conversations with Canadian Novelists* (Toronto: Macmillan, 1973), Pt. 1, p. 100. All further references to this work (Cameron) appear in the text.

[3] "Where the World Began," *Maclean's*, Dec. 1972, pp. 23, 80; rpt. (rev.) in *Heart of a Stranger* (Toronto: McClelland and Stewart, 1976), p. 217.

[4] "Jericho's Brick Battlements," in *A Bird in the House* (Toronto: McClelland and Stewart, 1970), p. 207. All further references to this work (*BH*) appear in the text. See also "Sources," *Mosaic*, 3, No. 3 (Spring 1970), 80–84; rpt. (rev.) "A Place to Stand On," in *Heart of a Stranger*, p. 17.

[5] Clara Thomas, *The Manawaka World of Margaret Laurence* (Toronto: McClelland and Stewart, 1975), pp. 13, 15. For a fuller account of Laurence's life, see this book and Susan J. Warwick, "A Laurence Log," *Journal of Canadian Studies*, 13, No. 3 (Fall 1978), 75–83.

[6] Margaret Laurence, "Ten Years' Sentences," *Canadian Literature*, No. 41 (Summer 1969), pp. 10–16; rpt. in *Margaret Laurence: The Writer and Her Critics*, ed. William H. New (Toronto: McGraw-Hill Ryerson, 1977), p. 20. All further references to this work appear in the text.

[7] Margaret Atwood, "Face to Face," *Maclean's*, May 1974, pp. 38–39, 43–46; rpt. in New, ed., *Margaret Laurence*, p. 34.

[8] Margaret Laurence, "A Statement of Faith," in *A Place to Stand On: Essays by and about Margaret Laurence*, ed. George Woodcock, Western Canadian Literary Documents, No. 4 (Edmonton: NeWest, 1983), p. 56.

[9] Bernice Lever, "Literature and Canadian Culture: An Interview with Margaret Laurence," *Alive*, No. 41 (1975), pp. 18–19; rpt. in New, ed., *Margaret Laurence*, p. 26.

[10] Michel Fabre, "From *The Stone Angel* to *The Diviners*: An Interview with Margaret Laurence," in Woodcock, ed., *A Place to Stand On*, p. 201; Margaret Laurence, "My Final Hour," *Canadian Literature*, No. 100 (Spring 1984), p. 196.

[11] Graeme Gibson, "Margaret Laurence," in *Eleven Canadian Novelists Interviewed by Graeme Gibson* (Toronto: House of Anansi, 1973), p. 194.

[12] Margaret Laurence, "A Canadian Classic?" rev. of *Jake and the Kid*, by W. O. Mitchell, *Canadian Literature*, No. 11 (Winter 1962), p. 68. See also her Introduction in *The Lamp at Noon and Other Stories*, by Sinclair Ross, New Canadian Library, No. 62 (Toronto: McClelland and Stewart, 1968), pp. 7–12.

[13] Robert Kroetsch, "A Conversation with Margaret Laurence," in *creation*, ed. Robert Kroetsch (Toronto: new, 1970), pp. 53, 54, 55.

[14] "The Pure Diamond Man," in *The Tomorrow-Tamer* (Toronto: McClelland and Stewart, 1963), p. 182. In all further references, this work is abbreviated as *TT*.

[15] *The Prophet's Camel Bell* (Toronto: McClelland and Stewart, 1963), p. 81.

[16] Margaret Laurence, "Caverns to the Mind's Dark Continent," rev. of *The New Ancestors*, by Dave Godfrey, *The Globe Magazine*, 5 Dec. 1970, p. 18.

[17] Margaret Laurence, "Ivory Tower or Grassroots?: The Novelist as Socio-Political Being," in *A Political Art: Essays and Images in Honour of George Woodcock*, ed. William H. New (Vancouver: Univ. of British

Columbia Press, 1978), p. 22. All further references to this work appear in the text.

[18] Atwood, p. 36.

[19] "The Rain Child," in *Winter's Tales 8*, ed. A. D. MacLean (New York: St. Martin's, 1962), pp. 105–42; rpt. in *TT*, pp. 105–33.

[20] Henry James, *The Art of the Novel*, ed. R. P. Blackmur (1934; rpt. New York: Scribner, 1962), pp. 129, 293, 289.

[21] Dick Harrison, *Unnamed Country: The Struggle for a Canadian Prairie Fiction* (Edmonton: Univ. of Alberta Press, 1977), p. 100 ff.

[22] Patricia Morley, *Margaret Laurence*, Twayne's World Authors Series, No. 591 (Boston: Twayne, 1981), p. 7.

[23] For the sake of clarity, in this section I will simply name the critics and refer readers to the bibliography. When essays appear in one of the four main collections of articles, I will indicate them through the following abbreviations: *ML*: New, ed., *Margaret Laurence*; *JCS*: Michael Peterman, ed. and introd., *Journal of Canadian Studies*, 13, No. 3 (Fall 1978); *JCF*: John R. Sorfleet, ed., *Journal of Canadian Fiction*, No. 27 (1980) [*The Work of Margaret Laurence*]; *EC*: Michel Fabre, ed., *Etudes Canadiennes*, No. 11 (1981) [The Stone Angel *by Margaret Laurence: A Collection of Essays*].

[24] Stephanie A. Demetrakopoulos, "Laurence's Fiction: A Revisioning of Feminine Archetypes," *Canadian Literature*, No. 93 (Summer 1983), p. 46.

[25] Thomas, p. 14.

[26] Margaret Laurence, Introd., *Above Ground*, by Jack Ludwig, New Canadian Library, No. 100 (Toronto: McClelland and Stewart, 1974), n. pag.

[27] *Long Drums and Cannons: Nigerian Dramatists and Novelists 1952–1966* (London: Macmillan, 1968), p. 122. All further references to this work (*LDC*) appear in the text.

[28] Margaret Laurence, "Gadgetry or Growing: Form and Voice in the Novel," *Journal of Canadian Fiction*, No. 27 (1980) [*The Work of Margaret Laurence*], p. 62.

[29] Margaret Laurence, "Roses and Yew," rev. of *Memoirs of Montparnasse*, by John Glassco, *The Tamarack Review*, No. 54 (Winter 1970), p. 80.

[30] Laurence, *The Prophet's Camel Bell*, p. 1.

[31] Bernice Lever, "Margaret Laurence, November 20, 1974," *Waves*, 3, No. 2 (Winter 1975), 7.

[32] Margaret Laurence, "African Experience," rev. of *Farquharson's Physique and What It Did to His Mind*, by David Knight, *Journal of Canadian Fiction*, 1, No. 1 (Winter 1972), 77.

[33] *This Side Jordan* (Toronto: McClelland and Stewart, 1960), p. 106. All further references to this work (*TSJ*) appear in the text.

[34] Margaret Laurence, "Time and the Narrative Voice," in *The Narrative Voice: Short Stories and Reflections by Canadian Writers*, ed. John Metcalf (Toronto: McGraw-Hill Ryerson, 1972), pp. 126–30; rpt. in New, ed., *Margaret Laurence*, p. 156. All further references to this work appear in the text.

[35] For discussion of Laurence's debt to Mannoni, see: Jane Leney, "Prospero and Caliban in Laurence's African Fiction," *Journal of Canadian Fiction*, No. 27 (1980) [*The Work of Margaret Laurence*], pp. 63–80; Patricia Morley, "The Long Trek Home: Margaret Laurence's Stories," *Journal of Canadian Studies*, 11, No. 4 (Nov. 1976), 19–26; George Woodcock, "Many Solitudes: The Travel Writings of Margaret Laurence," *Journal of Canadian Studies*, 13, No. 3 (Fall 1978), 3–12.

[36] Margaret Laurence, "Illusions of Simplicity," rev. of *Ask the Name of the Lion*, by Ralph Allen, *Canadian Literature*, No. 14 (Autumn 1962), p. 61.

[37] Gibson, p. 195.

[38] *The Stone Angel* (Toronto: McClelland and Stewart, 1964), p. 304. All further references to this work appear in the text.

[39] Kroetsch, p. 60.

[40] Laurence, "Gadgetry or Growing," p. 55.

[41] *A Jest of God* (Toronto: McClelland and Stewart, 1966), pp. 162–63. All further references to this work appear in the text.

[42] See esp. C. M. McLay, "Every Man Is an Island: Isolation in *A Jest of God*," *Canadian Literature*, No. 50 (Autumn 1971), pp. 57–68; rpt. in New, ed., *Margaret Laurence*, pp. 177–88.

[43] Margaret Laurence, "Listen. Just Listen," in *Divided We Stand*, ed. Gary Geddes (Toronto: Peter Martin, 1977), p. 25.

[44] *The Fire-Dwellers* (Toronto: McClelland and Stewart, 1969), p. 80. All further references to this work appear in the text.

[45] Theo Q. Dombrowski, "Who Is This You? Margaret Laurence and Identity," *The University of Windsor Review*, 13, No. 1 (Fall–Winter 1977), 33.

[46] Dombrowski, p. 22.

[47] George Steiner, "Eros and Idiom," in *On Difficulty and Other Essays* (Oxford: Oxford Univ. Press, 1978), p. 135.

[48] David L. Jeffrey, "Biblical Hermeneutic and Family History in Contemporary Canadian Fiction: Wiebe and Laurence," *Mosaic*, 11, No. 3 (Spring 1978), 89, 95.

[49] *The Diviners* (Toronto: McClelland and Stewart, 1974), p. 8. All further references to this work appear in the text.

[50] Margaret Laurence, "Stubborn Pride," rev. of *The Humback*, by Mort Forer, *The Tamarack Review*, No. 55 (Spring 1970), p. 79.

[51] Laurence, "Listen. Just Listen," pp. 20, 22.

[52] Alan Twigg, "Margaret Laurence: Canadian Literature," in *For Openers: Conversations with Twenty-Four Canadian Writers* (Madeira Park, B.C.: Harbour, 1981), p. 267.

[53] Margaret Laurence, Introd., *Crackpot*, by Adele Wiseman, New Canadian Library, No. 144 (Toronto: McClelland and Stewart, 1978), p. 4.

[54] *The Interpreter's Dictionary of the Bible*, s.v. "grace."

[55] Twigg, p. 267.

[56] Laurence, Introd., *Above Ground*, n. pag.

[57] Margaret Laurence, "Myth into Man," rev. of *Rizpah*, by Charles Israel, *Canadian Literature*, No. 9 (Summer 1961), p. 68.

[58] Kenneth C. Russell, "Margaret Laurence's Seekers after Grace," *The Chelsea Journal*, 3 (Sept.–Oct. 1977), 245, 247.

[59] Kenneth C. Russell, "God and Church in the Fiction of Margaret Laurence," *Studies in Religion/Sciences Réligieuses*, 7 (Fall 1978), 446.

SELECTED BIBLIOGRAPHY

Primary Sources

Books

Laurence, Margaret, ed. and trans. *A Tree for Poverty: Somali Poetry and Prose*. Nairobi: Eagle, 1954.

———. *This Side Jordan*. Toronto: McClelland and Stewart, 1960.

———. *The Prophet's Camel Bell*. Toronto: McClelland and Stewart, 1963.

———. *The Tomorrow-Tamer*. Toronto: McClelland and Stewart, 1963.

———. *The Stone Angel*. Toronto: McClelland and Stewart, 1964.

———. *A Jest of God*. Toronto: McClelland and Stewart, 1966.

———. *Long Drums and Cannons: Nigerian Dramatists and Novelists 1952–1966*. London: Macmillan, 1968.

———. *The Fire-Dwellers*. Toronto: McClelland and Stewart, 1969.

———. *A Bird in the House*. Toronto: McClelland and Stewart, 1970.

———. *Jason's Quest*. Toronto: McClelland and Stewart, 1970.

———. *The Diviners*. Toronto: McClelland and Stewart, 1974.

———. *Heart of a Stranger*. Toronto: McClelland and Stewart, 1976.

———. *The Olden Days Coat*. Toronto: McClelland and Stewart, 1979.

———. *Six Darn Cows*. Toronto: James Lorimer, 1979.

———. *The Christmas Birthday Story*. Toronto: McClelland and Stewart, 1980.

Contributions to Periodicals and Books

Laurence, Margaret. "Myth into Man." Rev. of *Rizpah*, by Charles Israel. *Canadian Literature*, No. 9 (Summer 1961), pp. 68–69.

———. "A Canadian Classic?" Rev. of *Jake and the Kid*, by W. O. Mitchell. *Canadian Literature*, No. 11 (Winter 1962), pp. 68–70.

———. "Illusions of Simplicity." Rev. of *Ask the Name of the Lion*, by Ralph Allen. *Canadian Literature*, No. 14 (Autumn 1962), pp. 57–62.

———, introd. *The Lamp at Noon and Other Stories*. By Sinclair Ross. New Canadian Library, No. 62. Toronto: McClelland and Stewart, 1968, pp. 7–12.

———. "Ten Years' Sentences." *Canadian Literature*, No. 41 (Summer 1969), pp. 10–16. Rpt. in *Margaret Laurence: The Writer and Her Critics*. Ed. William H. New. Toronto: McGraw-Hill Ryerson, 1977, pp. 17–32.

———. "Roses and Yew." Rev. of *Memoirs of Montparnasse*, by John Glassco. *The Tamarack Review*, No. 54 (Winter 1970), pp. 77–80.

———. "Stubborn Pride." Rev. of *The Humback*, by Mort Forer. *The Tamarack Review*, No. 55 (Spring 1970), pp. 77–79.

———. "Caverns to the Mind's Dark Continent." Rev. of *The New Ancestors*, by Dave Godfrey. *The Globe Magazine*, 5 Dec. 1970, p. 18.

———. "African Experience." Rev. of *Farquharson's Physique and What It Did to His Mind*, by David Knight. *Journal of Canadian Fiction*, 1, No. 1 (Winter 1972), 77–78.

———. "Time and the Narrative Voice." In *The Narrative Voice: Short Stories and Reflections by Canadian Writers*. Ed. John Metcalf. Toronto: McGraw-Hill Ryerson, 1972, pp. 126–30. Rpt. in *Margaret Laurence: The Writer and Her Critics*. Ed. William H. New. Toronto: McGraw-Hill Ryerson, 1977, pp. 156–60.

———, introd. *Above Ground*. By Jack Ludwig. New Canadian Library, No. 100. Toronto: McClelland and Stewart, 1974, n. pag.

———, introd. *House of Hate*. By Percy Janes. New Canadian Library, No. 124. Toronto: McClelland and Stewart, 1976, pp. vii–xi.

———. "Listen. Just Listen." In *Divided We Stand*. Ed. Gary Geddes. Toronto: Peter Martin, 1977, pp. 20–25.

———, introd. *Crackpot*. By Adele Wiseman. New Canadian Library, No. 144. Toronto: McClelland and Stewart, 1978, pp. 3–8.

———. "Ivory Tower or Grassroots?: The Novelist as Socio-Political Being." In *A Political Art: Essays and Images in Honour of George Woodcock*. Ed. William H. New. Vancouver: Univ. of British Columbia Press, 1978, pp. 15–25.

———. "Gadgetry or Growing: Form and Voice in the Novel." *Journal of Canadian Fiction*, No. 27 (1980) [*The Work of Margaret Laurence*], pp. 54–62.

———. "A Statement of Faith." In *A Place to Stand On: Essays by and about Margaret Laurence*. Ed. George Woodcock. Western Canadian Literary Documents, No. 4. Edmonton: NeWest, 1983, pp. 56–60.

———. "My Final Hour." *Canadian Literature*, No. 100 (Spring 1984), pp. 187–97.

Secondary Sources

Atwood, Margaret. *Survival: A Thematic Guide to Canadian Literature.* Toronto: House of Anansi, 1972.

———. "Face to Face." *Maclean's*, May 1974, pp. 38–39, 43–46. Rpt. in *Margaret Laurence: The Writer and Her Critics*. Ed. William H. New. Toronto: McGraw-Hill Ryerson, 1977, pp. 33–40.

Bailey, Nancy. "Margaret Laurence, Carl Jung and the Manawaka Women." *Studies in Canadian Literature*, 2 (Summer 1977), 306–21.

Burton, Lydia, and David Morley. "A Sense of Grievance: Attitudes toward Men in Contemporary Fiction." *The Canadian Forum*, Sept. 1975, pp. 57–60.

Buss, Helen M. *Mother and Daughter Relationships in the Manawaka Novels of Margaret Laurence*. Victoria: Univ. of Victoria Press, 1985.

Cameron, Donald. "Margaret Laurence: The Black Celt Speaks of Freedom." In *Conversations with Canadian Novelists*. Toronto: Macmillan, 1973. Pt. 1, pp. 96–115.

Carrington, Ildikó de Papp. "'Tales in the Telling': *The Diviners* as a Fiction about Fiction." *Essays on Canadian Writing*, No. 9 (Winter 1977–78), pp. 154–69.

Cooley, Dennis. "Antimacassared in the Wilderness: Art and Nature in *The Stone Angel*." *Mosaic*, 11, No. 3 (Spring 1978), 29–46.

Cooper, Cheryl. "Images of Closure in *The Diviners*." In *The Canadian Novel: Here and Now*. Ed. John Moss. Toronto: NC, 1978, pp. 93–102.

Davidson, Cathy N. "Geography and Psychology in the Manitoba Fiction of Margaret Laurence." *Kate Chopin Newsletter*, 2, No. 2 (1976), 5–10.

———. "Past and Perspective in Margaret Laurence's *The Stone Angel*." *The American Review of Canadian Studies*, 8, No. 2 (Autumn 1978), 61–69.

Demetrakopoulos, Stephanie A. "Laurence's Fiction: A Revisioning of Feminine Archetypes." *Canadian Literature*, No. 93 (Summer 1983), pp. 42–57.

Djwa, Sandra. "Biblical Archetypes in Western Canadian Fiction." In *Western Canada: Past and Present*. Ed. Anthony Rasporich. Toronto: McClelland and Stewart, 1975, pp. 193–203.

Dombrowski, Theo Q. "Who Is This You? Margaret Laurence and

Identity." *The University of Windsor Review*, 13, No. 1 (Fall–Winter 1977), 21–38.

Fabre, Michel, ed. *Etudes Canadiennes*, No. 11 (1981) [The Stone Angel *by Margaret Laurence: A Collection of Critical Essays*].

———. "Words and the World: *The Diviners* as an Exploration of the Book of Life." *Canadian Literature*, No. 93 (Summer 1982), pp. 60–78. Rpt. in *A Place to Stand On: Essays by and about Margaret Laurence*. Ed. George Woodcock. Western Canadian Literary Documents, No. 4. Edmonton: NeWest, 1983, pp. 247–69.

———. "From *The Stone Angel* to *The Diviners*: An Interview with Margaret Laurence." In *A Place to Stand On: Essays by and about Margaret Laurence*. Ed. George Woodcock. Western Canadian Literary Documents, No. 4. Edmonton: NeWest, 1983, pp. 193–209.

Gibson, Graeme. "Margaret Laurence." In *Eleven Canadian Novelists Interviewed by Graeme Gibson*. Toronto: House of Anansi, 1973, pp. 181–208.

Gom, Leona. "Margaret Laurence and the First Person." *Dalhousie Review*, 55 (Summer 1975), 235–51.

———. "Margaret Laurence: The Importance of Place." *West Coast Review*, 10, No. 2 (Oct. 1975), 26–30.

———. "Laurence and the Use of Memory." *Canadian Literature*, No. 71 (Winter 1976), pp. 48–58.

Gottlieb, Lois, and Wendy Keitner. "Mothers and Daughters in Four Recent Canadian Novels." *The Sphinx*, No. 4 (Summer 1975), pp. 21–34.

Grace, Sherrill. "Crossing Jordan: Time and Memory in the Fiction of Margaret Laurence." *World Literature Written in English*, 16 (Nov. 1977), 328–39.

Harrison, Dick. *Unnamed Country: The Struggle for a Canadian Prairie Fiction*. Edmonton: Univ. of Alberta Press, 1977.

Hehner, Barbara. "River of Now and Then: Margaret Laurence's Narratives." *Canadian Literature*, No. 74 (Autumn 1977), pp. 40–57.

Hind-Smith, Joan. *Three Voices*. Toronto: Clarke, Irwin, 1975.

Hutcheon, Linda. "Atwood and Laurence: Poet and Novelist." *Studies in Canadian Literature*, 3 (Summer 1978), 255–63.

James, Henry. *The Art of the Novel*. Ed. R. P. Blackmur. 1934; rpt. New York: Scribner, 1962.

Jeffrey, David L. "Biblical Hermeneutic and Family History in Contemporary Canadian Fiction: Wiebe and Laurence." *Mosaic*, 11, No. 3 (Spring 1978), 87–106.

Johnston, Eleanor. "The Quest of *The Diviners*." *Mosaic*, 11, No. 3 (Spring

1978), 107–17.
Jones, D. G. *Butterfly on Rock: A Study of Themes and Images in Canadian Literature*. Toronto: Univ. of Toronto Press, 1970.
Kertzer, J. M. "*The Stone Angel*: Time and Responsibility." *Dalhousie Review*, 54 (Autumn 1974), 499–509.
Killam, G. D., introd. *A Jest of God*. New Canadian Library, No. 111. Toronto: McClelland and Stewart, 1974, n. pag.
———, introd. *This Side Jordan*. New Canadian Library, No. 126. Toronto: McClelland and Stewart, 1976, pp. ix–xviii.
Kroetsch, Robert. "A Conversation with Margaret Laurence." In *creation*. Ed. Robert Kroetsch. Toronto: new, 1970, pp. 53–63.
Leney, Jane. "Prospero and Caliban in Laurence's African Fiction," *Journal of Canadian Fiction*, No. 27 (1980) [*The Work of Margaret Laurence*], pp. 63–80.
Lever, Bernice. "Margaret Laurence, November 20, 1974" [interview]. *Waves*, 3, No. 2 (Winter 1975), 4–12.
———. "Literature and Canadian Culture: An Interview with Margaret Laurence." *Alive*, No. 41 (1975), pp. 18–19. Rpt. in *Margaret Laurence: The Writer and Her Critics*. Ed. William H. New. Toronto: McGraw-Hill Ryerson, 1977, pp. 24–32.
———. "Nature Imagery in the Canadian Fiction of Margaret Laurence." *Alive*, No. 41 (1975), pp. 20–22.
McCourt, Edward. *The Canadian West in Fiction*. Rev. ed. Toronto: Ryerson, 1970.
McKenna, Isabel. "Women in Canadian Literature." *Canadian Literature*, No. 62 (Autumn 1974), pp. 69–78.
McLay, C. M. "Every Man Is an Island: Isolation in *A Jest of God*." *Canadian Literature*, No. 50 (Autumn 1971), pp. 57–68. Rpt. in *Margaret Laurence: The Writer and Her Critics*. Ed. William H. New. Toronto: McGraw-Hill Ryerson, 1977, pp. 177–88.
Monk, Patricia. "Shadow Continent: The Image of Africa in Three Canadian Writers." *Ariel*, 8, No. 4 (Oct. 1977), 3–25.
Morley, Patricia. "The Long Trek Home: Margaret Laurence's Stories." *Journal of Canadian Studies*, 11, No. 4 (Nov. 1976), 19–26.
———. *Margaret Laurence*. Twayne's World Authors Series, No. 591. Boston: Twayne, 1981.
Moss, John. *Patterns of Isolation in English Canadian Fiction*. Toronto: McClelland and Stewart, 1974.
———. *Sex and Violence in the Canadian Novel: The Ancestral Present*. Toronto: McClelland and Stewart, 1977.

New, William H. *Among Worlds: An Introduction to Modern Commonwealth and South African Fiction*. Erin, Ont.: Porcépic, 1975.

———. "Fiction." In *Literary History of Canada: Canadian Literature in English*. 2nd ed. Gen. ed. and introd. Carl F. Klinck. Toronto: Univ. of Toronto Press, 1976. III, 233–83.

———, ed. *Margaret Laurence: The Writer and Her Critics*. Toronto: McGraw-Hill Ryerson, 1977.

———. "Every Now and Then: Voice and Language in Laurence's *The Stone Angel*." *Canadian Literature*, No. 93 (Summer 1982), pp. 79–96. Rpt. in *A Place to Stand On: Essays by and about Margaret Laurence*. Ed. George Woodcock. Western Canadian Literary Documents, No. 4. Edmonton: NeWest, 1983, pp. 171–92.

Pesando, Frank. "In a Nameless Land: The Use of Apocalyptic Mythology in the Writing of Margaret Laurence." *Journal of Canadian Fiction*, 2, No. 1 (Winter 1973), 53–58.

Peterman, Michael, ed. and introd. *Journal of Canadian Studies*, 13, No. 3 (Fall 1978).

Pollack, Claudette. "The Paradox of *The Stone Angel*." *The Humanities Association Review*, 27 (Summer 1976), 267–75.

Ricou, Laurence. *Vertical Man/Horizontal World: Man and Landscape in Canadian Prairie Fiction*. Vancouver: Univ. of British Columbia Press, 1973.

Rooke, Constance. "A Feminist Reading of *The Stone Angel*." *Canadian Literature*, No. 93 (Summer 1982), pp. 26–41.

Russell, Kenneth C. "Margaret Laurence's Seekers after Grace." *The Chelsea Journal*, 3 (Sept.–Oct. 1977), 245–48.

———. "God and Church in the Fiction of Margaret Laurence." *Studies in Religion/Sciences Réligieuses*, 7 (Fall 1978), 435–46.

Sorfleet, John R., ed. *Journal of Canadian Fiction*, No. 27 (1980) [*The Work of Margaret Laurence*].

Steiner, George. *On Difficulty and Other Essays*. Oxford: Oxford Univ. Press, 1978.

Sullivan, Rosemary. "An Interview with Margaret Laurence." In *A Place to Stand On: Essays by and about Margaret Laurence*. Ed. George Woodcock. Western Canadian Literary Documents, No. 4. Edmonton: NeWest, 1983, pp. 61–79.

Swayze, Walter. "The Odyssey of Margaret Laurence." *The English Quarterly*, 3, No. 3 (Fall 1970), 7–17.

Thomas, Clara. "Happily Ever After: Canadian Women in Fiction and Fact." *Canadian Literature*, No. 34 (Autumn 1967), pp. 43–53.

——— . *Margaret Laurence*. Toronto: McClelland and Stewart, 1969.

——— . "Proud Lineage: Willa Cather and Margaret Laurence." *Canadian Review of American Studies*, 2, No. 1 (Spring 1971), 3–12.

——— . "A Conversation about Literature: An Interview with Margaret Laurence and Irving Layton." *Journal of Canadian Fiction*, 1, No. 1 (Winter 1972), 65–69.

——— . "The Short Stories of Margaret Laurence." *World Literature Written in English*, 2, No. 1 (1972), 25–33.

——— . *The Manawaka World of Margaret Laurence*. Toronto: McClelland and Stewart, 1975.

——— . "The Wild Garden and the Manawaka World." *Modern Fiction Studies*, 22 (Autumn 1976), 401–11.

——— . "Women Writers and the New Land." In *The New Land: Studies in a Literary Theme*. Ed. R. Chadbourne and H. Dahlie. Waterloo: Wilfred Laurier Univ. Press, 1978, pp. 45–59.

Thompson, Anne. "The Wilderness of Pride: Form and Image in *The Stone Angel*." *Journal of Canadian Fiction*, 4, No. 3 (Summer 1975), 95–110.

Twigg, Alan. "Margaret Laurence: Canadian Literature." In *For Openers: Conversations with Twenty-Four Canadian Writers*. Madeira Park, B.C.: Harbour, 1981, pp. 261–71.

Warwick, Susan J. "A Laurence Log." *Journal of Canadian Studies*, 13, No. 3 (Fall 1978), 75–83.

——— . "Margaret Laurence: An Annotated Bibliography." In *The Annotated Bibliography of Canada's Major Authors*. Ed. Robert Lecker and Jack David. Vol. 1. Downsview, Ont.: ECW, 1979, 47–101.

Woodcock, George. "Possessing the Land: Notes on Canadian Fiction." In *The Canadian Imagination: Dimensions of a Literary Culture*. Ed. David Staines. Cambridge, Mass.: Harvard Univ. Press, 1977, pp. 69–96.

——— . "Many Solitudes: The Travel Writings of Margaret Laurence." *Journal of Canadian Studies*, 13, No. 3 (Fall 1978), 3–12.

——— , ed. *A Place to Stand On: Essays by and about Margaret Laurence*. Western Canadian Literary Documents, No. 4. Edmonton: NeWest, 1983.